Gilbert Brands

Introduction to Computer Science

A Textbook for Beginners in Informatics

Dr. Gilbert Brands

D-26736 Krummhörn

Email: gilbert@gilbertbrands.de

ISBN-13: 978-1492827849

ISBN-10: 1492827843

2nd revised edition

The Reader is invited to join a forum on http://www.gilbertbrands.de/smf/ on questions, comments, or recommendations for further editions

Inhaltsverzeichnis

1 Which Technology for Computer Construction ?

1.1 Preliminary Remarks

Informatics or Computer Science is comprised of a lot of different disciplines, which cover in their basic lectures merely the same features. To avoid the situation that every lecturer has to repeat what has probably been lectured by his colleague (and will be repeated again by other colleagues) a special course "Introduction to Informatics" or "Introduction to Computer Science" is often provided by the universities.

In this short textbook we will cover the common basics for the specialized disciplines of computer science, as well hardware oriented as software disciplines. We will do it from a special point of view, namely from developing the basics from the questions "how can we do it?", and "why to do it in exactly that manner?". As the reader will see, there is a logical base for the construction of computers and their software, and there is no mystic engineering science in it.

Developing the principles from these questions is like grabbing in history, and some lectures on this theme restrict themselves to narrate about the early days of computer science. In this textbook, however, the history will not develop to more than a few footnotes. A reader expecting interesting stories about early IBM or Zuse computers should search for another textbook. The target here is to detect the scientific principles of computers and to have a short insight in modern application mechanisms.

As this textbook shall only be a starter for further studies (which will be presented to students in other courses), we will stop our discussion at some early point although one or another of the reader may feel that I'm going already into rather complex details in one or another field, others only touching softly. As I have my preferred working fields myself, I will not deny that some themes are discussed to greater depth.

In order to promote the understanding, I include some exercises. In the beginning, when I can go into some depth, there will be more exercises than later on when topics are touched in a more narrative kind. Solutions are not given here, but the reader may feel free to contact me by email if an exercise cannot be solved or there remain doubts about the correctness.

Last remark: a lecture with these contents is held by me at a German university, and German is my native language. I ask the English-speaking reader to be lenient if one or the other phrasing should sound a little weird.

1.2   Physical Basis of a Computer

So let's start! The first thing we should ask ourselves is: what should be the main features of a computer. As we do not have in mind a special task our computer shall solve, there are two main features to be considered:

1. **Universality.** As we know from mechanics, a tool may be used in different ways. It may be difficult to develop a new application scheme for a specific task, but this is in merely all cases far easier than to develop a completely new tool. So our computer shall solve most problems with the same hardware, the software (=program) as equivalent of the application scheme however may vary widely and accordingly.

2. **Scalability.** When using a computer as a private home calculation device, computing with some 100,000 $ will be sufficient in most cases, but using it in the Federal Reserve Bank calculations are done on a scale of 1,000,000,000,000 $. Some tasks at least require different precisions in numbers, and the machine must be scalable accordingly.

Similarly if the reader manages his friends, 100 memory locations may be enough, but that is not the case for a telephone company which may have millions of customers. Our computer, therefore, must also be scalable in memory space.

Scalability is a mixed problem of hardware, and software, as we see, but as far as hardware is concerned, the needed property should be accomplished by standard tools in an easy manor.

If we examine possible construction principles of a computer, we have to prove whether they fulfill these features. Starting from scratch we can estimate a

- pure mechanical computer(with some electric parts like motors to relieve human workers), or

- electrical computers (with some mechanic parts however) using

  ○ analogue signals (current or voltage), or

  ○ digital signals which differ from analog signals in only a few allowed analog levels corresponding to well defined digits, and in combining several of these digits to a well defined number.

A pure mechanical construction of a computer fulfilling our "must bes" is most probably possible when we have a look into history. The first computers, if we label them already with this name, used in the second world war were mechanical machines, but they were only constructed for a very special task (namely to break the German enigma cipher machine). Others were used in the Manhattan Project to calculate the optimal geometry of atomic bombs. They were at least "not very" universal or scalable, but a look at other very sophisticated mechanical machines tells us that a lot more is possible, although nobody really tried it in practice.

The next computer generation, which was developed after the first mechanical trials, was constructed on electrical means because

- the construction was easier,

- the machines were smaller and easier to maintain,

- they were more robust than their mechanical analogues,

- and – the main reason – they were far more faster than the mechanicals.

Mechanical solutions were, therefore, discarded, and the engineers concentrated on the development of electrical machines.

The next step in the development line was to discriminate between analogue and digital construction principles. In principle this applies also to mechanical machines, but implicitly I assumed digital constructions, which was caused by their areas of application.

In analogue signal processing, the voltage may represent directly a certain value, for instance the number 4.54 is represented directly by 4.54 V, and if we add the number 3.30, the output should be 7.84 V. But if we square this number, the expected value is 61.4656 V, and if we have a short look at a voltage meter, this is already 1-2 digits to much for our measurement equipment. So just two steps from the start we have to recognize: analogue computers have a severe problem with the scalability principle.

If we follow the line further, we would also recognize that analogue computers also violate the universality principle. They are wonderful machines to solve very fast certain problems of coupled differential equations if the reduced precision of 1% of the output values is sufficient, but we are forced to discard them like mechanical solutions in out further investigations.

So we concentrate on digital signal processing. Is it possible to restrict this idea further? Let's have a look on some possibilities:

We are accustomed to calculate on the base of the number 10 (which is not compelling: south American natives used the number 60, ancient people of Mesopotamia or Egypt did so, too, and in China different counting systems are used) due to our ten fingers (except workers in a sawmill), which are used as some kind of primitive calculation mechanics. Starting from our fingers, a possible digital system may assign the voltages

$$0 - 1 - 2 - 3 - 4 - 5 - 6 - 7 - 8 - 9 \quad (\pm\ 0.1\ V)$$

to the appropriate digits, , and if adding of two numbers (= two voltages) represented by one digit each results in an output of 15 V, the
result is split up to two combined voltage lines of 1 V, and 5 V respectively.

This approach has several disadvantages if we transform the theory to
practice. We have for instance to observe that this is a mix of analogue, and digital computation, and we have to admit that a voltage
interval of

```
0.9 .. 1.1 V
```

represents the number 1. Adding 5 times the number one without
correction between the operations has in worst case the result 4.5 V.
Now, what is the exact result? 4 oder 5? If we would follow this development line, further difficulties would show up.

So again from very basic assumptions we arrive at the conclusion that
digital computing should be done on few digits. Our number system
using ten digits may be dangerous up from the beginning because of a
low fault tolerance of a mixed analogue/digital system.

The most simple system would use only 2 digits, namely 0, and 1,
represented by 0 V (no voltage), and for instance 5 V (battery voltage), and because a split test is necessary after each computation step,
the result should remain exact even in long and complicated computations with many digits.

If we would follow the multiple digit strategy nevertheless, whether
base on the base number 10 or something else, and compare it to the
two digit solution, which will be (partly) presented later in the book,
we would also recognize that the two digit solution comes at an easier
hardware solution too.

Isn't it fascinating how fast we arrive at the construction principle of
modern digital computers only using two main principles, and some
experimental facts, and a few logical conclusions? But as far as now, a
computer using only 0, and 1 can primarily only answer questions
giving the answer YES or NO, and we have to show – besides some
hardware construction possibilities – that YES or NO is sufficient to
do all calculations we can do on paper with a pencil. So let's go on
with YES, and NO.

2   Binary (Boolean) Logic

This chapter deals with the mathematics of binary logic, and how to realize logics on electronic chips along with some other electronic circuits needed. A short introduction on semiconductor principles is included, too. It's nearly all background information, and if the reader don't want to assemble electronic chips to some functional boards himself, he will hardly get into contact with this matter in the future. I recommend the reader to work through the chapter nevertheless, because background information is often helpful.

2.1   Logical Expressions

As we have deduced, the smallest units of our computers can only have one of two possible states, namely 0 or 1, or YES or NO, or TRUE or FALSE. These are the states of expressive logics, which may be discussed in depth in the math course. We will nevertheless present a little bit theory, because this is necessary to understand the following chapters.

An expression in the common sense is a sentence like "it is raining". The evaluation of an expression is either TRUE oder FALSE, depending on the weather conditions outside in this example. The evaluation may change on waiting some time, but this will be of no interest in our considerations. Mathematicians investigate such situations in special theories of temporal logics, and similar uncertainties in life may be called "female logic", and are investigated by comedians. Here, we restrict to the simplest case, and the time "now".

Operators are used to combine the states of several expressions to a composed state, which can also be TRUE or FALSE, for instance

```
"it is raining" AND "the street is wet"
```

If both is true, the outcome of the combination with the operator AND is true too; if for instance the street is wet, but raining has stopped already, this combination will result in the evaluation FALSE, because both things don't happen simultaneously. The operator AND asks for conditions that are true at the same time.

This is the mathematical definition of the operator AND, and it is used by most people in conversation in this significance. If I ask for the definition in a greater audience however there are some small deviations sometime, not quite for the definition of AND but surely for other operators. To arrive at a clear theory the mathematicians had to fix the definition definitively, and we use the operators exactly in the mathematic sense. If a reader has some other understanding of certain operators, he has to suppress this at least when dealing with informatics.

Besides, it is an interesting observation that small children use logical linkages in the mathematical sense which seems to be the natural way of linking expressions, therefore. The mentiones deviations arrive at later times, and are due to cultural customs.

Theoretically an operator can work on arbitrary many input states. How many operators are needed to describe all cases of a combinations theoretically possible? If we look, for example, at only 3 expressions each being either TRUE or FALSE, the reader may count with a little effort that there are 8 different input combinations possible:

```
1:   FALSE    FALSE    FALSE
2:   FALSE    FALSE    TRUE
. . . .
8:   TRUE     TRUE     TRUE
```

Each input can have TRUE or FALSE for an arbitrary operator operating on 3 inputs, and each operator has one of theses outputs for every input combination.

```
        1 2 3 4 5 6 7 8
      -----------------------
OP_1:   F F F F F F F F
OP_2:   F F F F F F F T
. . . .
OP_n:   T T T T T T T T
```

If all output possibilities on different input signals should be fulfilled, we get a number of 256 different operators necessary to work on 3 input states.

This is surely a theoretical consideration. In reality nobody would really need all operators. But our computer should be universal, therefore, we have to investigate the question, whether it is possible to to solve every problem theoretical conceivable with only a small and fixed number of different operators.

2.1.1   Unary Operator

The simplest, and only one technical interesting unary operator – an operator operating on just one input – is the negation, which inverts the state of an expression:

$$A(=TRUE) \quad \text{converts to} \quad \neg A(=FALSE)$$

From a theoretical point of view three further operators can be defined:

- the identity operator, leaving the value unchanged,
- the erase operator resulting always in FALSE, and
- the creation operator giving always TRUE.

These operators are interesting only for the theorist, not in our practice. The reader may, however, be confronted with these operators in a math lecture. For a more humorist explanation of the erase and creation operators see .OP. and .SP. operators in the next chapters.

2.1.2   Binary Operators

Binary operators act on two expressions, and the mathematical syntax is

$$A.op.B$$

To explain the assessment of the number of operators in case of three inputs, we list the possible outputs for the four different input combinations of a binary operator in a table, and we observe that there are 16 possible results, and, therefore, 16 conceivable operators, each leading to another combination of output values depending on the input combination:

I	Output															
00	0	1	0	0	0	1	1	1	0	0	0	1	1	1	1	1
01	0	0	1	0	0	1	0	0	1	1	0	1	0	1	1	1
10	0	0	0	1	0	0	1	0	1	0	1	1	1	0	1	1
11	0	0	0	0	1	0	0	1	0	1	1	0	1	1	0	1

To systematize the calculation, the reader may figure out that a n -ary operator has 2^n different input states, and the possible bit patterns corresponding to the possible operators in the output combinations counts up to

$$2^{(2^n)}$$

Not all of these 16 operators are represented by terms of daily language. Widely used, but not being explicitly aware of this circumstance are the first and the last, known as .OP. , and .SP. Operators. They are especially used in politics, where the   .OP.   or "Other_Party" operator guarantees that statement combinations of the political opponent are always false, while the   .SP.   or "Same_Party" operator takes care that statements of party contemporaries turn out to be true, regardless what they will dowel. These operators play no role elsewhere. ☺

Some of the other operators, however, are well known in our daily language and in mathematical logics. In the following table, the last row contains the so called "truth table" of the operator result, which contains the input values of A in the first row, and the input values of B in the first line.

Operation	Symbolic	Table		
A and B	$A \wedge B$	**A/B**	**0**	**1**
		0	0	0
		1	0	1
A or B	$A \vee B$	**A/B**	**0**	**1**
		0	0	1
		1	1	1
if A then B from A follows B	$A \Rightarrow B$	**A/B**	**0**	**1**
		0	1	1
		1	0	1
A equivalent to B A exactly when B	$A \Leftrightarrow B$	**A/B**	**0**	**1**
		0	1	0
		1	0	1
Either A or B	A .XOR. B	**A/B**	**0**	**1**
		0	0	1
		1	1	0
Neither A nor B	A .NI. B	**A/B**	**0**	**1**
		0	1	0
		1	0	0

If you look around for a while, you can find probably more operators identifiable in daily language, and circuit technology. I restricted the examples here to operators, which are well defined by mathematical symbols or used in programming languages.

Exercise. Try to find examples for expressions and operations in daily speech. Try to identify further operators and construct their truth tables.

As the reader may have recognized, therefore, many of these operators are commutative, which means that the operands A, and B may change their position in the operation without changing the output. Other operators like $\Rightarrow$ are not commutative. This is easy to discover: if the 2x2 truth table of an operator is symmetrical to the diagonal, the operator is commutative, otherwise not.

Perhaps a little bit surprising in the first moment if you never had been in contact with mathematical logic, may be the truth table of the **if .. then ..** operator (it may be that this feeling applies also to the mathematical defined outcome of some other operators): if A in the expression $A \Rightarrow B$ is in the FALSE state, the state of B is arbitrary, and the output is always TRUE, meaning: from a false start condition every conclusion made is true. Emotionally, one would probably think that a conclusion from a false condition mus also be false, but math now tells us something else.

To understand that, think again a little bit about politics, and you will notice that there is no reason to wonder about: politicians often start with an arbitrary (and mostly wrong) assertion, and always claim afterwards that his conclusion about an even arbitrary outcome is true ☺.

But back to science! If we play around a little with different operator combinations, and construct their truth tables, we will get the following interesting equivalences:

$$((A \wedge B) \vee (\neg A \wedge \neg B)) \quad \Leftrightarrow \quad (A \Leftrightarrow B)$$

$$(\neg A \vee B) \quad \Leftrightarrow \quad (A \Rightarrow B)$$

$$(\neg(\neg A \wedge \neg B)) \quad \Leftrightarrow \quad (A \vee B)$$

Exercise. Verify these formulas. An example of the verification process is represented by the following table.

A	B	$A \wedge B$	$\neg A$	$\neg B$	$\neg A \wedge \neg B$	$X \vee Y$	$A \Leftrightarrow B$
0	0	0	1	1	1	1	1
0	1	0	1	0	0	0	0
1	0	0	0	1	0	0	0
1	1	1	0	0	0	1	1

We observe: some of the operators can be substituted by a combination of other binary and the unary operator. The total output table consists of 16 operators, but for the realization of all possible outcomes we don't need all 16.

How many do we really need? To give a first answer, solve the following exercise:

Excercise. Show that all 16 possible operators can be represented by a combination of NOT, AND, OR, IF..THEN.., and EQUIVA-LENT.

A set of operators, which can simulate all 16 possible operators, is called a complete set. As we have shown already that conclusion, and equivalence can be expressed by $\neg \wedge \vee$, and further OR by using AND, and NOT, $\neg \wedge$ is sufficient for expressing all possible binary logical conclusions, and is, therefore, a complete system.

There are even smaller ones:

Exercise. Show that

$$(A.\mathit{ni}.B) \;\Leftrightarrow\; (\neg A \wedge \neg B) \;\; \text{and}$$

$$(A.\mathit{nand}.B) \;\Leftrightarrow\; \neg(A \wedge B)$$

are complete systems *including the unary operator.*

Good news for our computer construction. As far as only unary and binary operations are concerned, **one single circuit can do the job,** perhaps in some complicated circuit designs.

Note. The reader may have had yet her first exercises in the programming course. Programming languages restrict the defined logical op-

erators to AND, OR, XOR, and NOT, but in two different ways as
logical operators, and bitwise operators. We come back to this later
on.

Note. In some languages questions like "wouldn't you eat your soup?"
are normally answered by "no" if the person asked doesn't want to eat
it. Form a logical point of view the correct answer should be "yes (,i
do not wand to eat my soup)" where the second part is normally sup-
pressed in the answer. This is one of the cultural influences on the
common understanding of logics. "Wouldn't you eat your soup?" is
more polite than "eat your damned soup NOW!", but that is exactly
what is meant and understood, and from this meaning the answer
"no" is correct again. This example surely doesn't fit to all languages,
but the reader may surely find other examples of such shifts in meaning.

2.1.3   Ternary, and higher operators

> **Exercise.** We leave it to the reader to show that all higher opera-
> tors can always be represented by a term only containing binary
> and unary operators.
>
> The most simple way is to describe each TRUE bit at the output
> by an AND concatenation of the corresponding TRUE input val-
> ues and the negated FALSE input bits, giving only this input com-
> bination a TRUE output. All these combinations are concate-
> nated by OR.

This method isn't very elegant and will produce in most cases far
longer terms than are necessary. If you are not content with a solution, nobody will discourage you to optimize a certain situation. The
most important conclusion for our main problem is: **no higher operators than binary ones are necessary to solve any arbitrary
logical problems.**

2.1.4   Conclusion

As far as our computer construction is concerned, we may assess that one single circuit design, for instance NAND, is all we need. If engineers construct other logical circuits, this may result in faster calculation and simpler hardware, but there is no reason why the computer construction should fail.

There is a lot more to say about logical operations. Exist preferable "normal presentations" of a complex operation? And if so, what are the basic laws, the algebra, to construct a normal presentation for an arbitrary logical expression? The answers to these questions are as important for circuit construction as for database implementation, and are topics of other lectures.

Besides the discussed boolean logic or boolean algebra, predicate logic operates on sets where all, one, or no element fulfill a certain condition. Such logics are also needed in computer science, but will be topics of other special courses in database construction or computer linguistics. We leave that to these lectures, and stop here with the theory of logics.

What remains to do? Two things:

- We have to show how to construct computer hardware operating on logical circuits.

- We have to show how to perform calculations with numbers on top of logical circuits.

2.2   Circuits for boolean logics

2.2.1   Some Computer History

Is it possible to construct electrical circuits, which realize a complete set of logical operators only using a battery, resistors, diodes, transistors, and wire?

Figure 2.1: computer with electronic valves as computing elements

Of course it is, when we look at history, and the first electronic calculators were already constructed in then pre-semiconductor time using electron valves. They were built-in in an accessible cabinet, which could have been used as sauna inside because of the heat of the valves (Figure 2.1). The heat was one limiting factor of building larger computers.

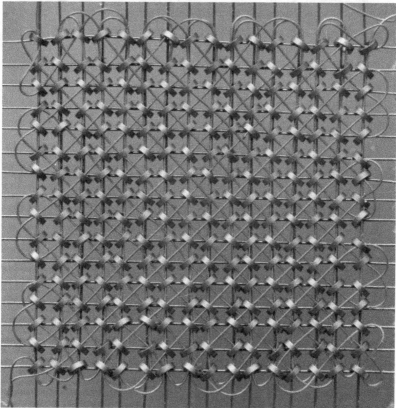

Figure 2.2: magentic memory grid

But logical circuits are not the only device necessary. Information has to be stored somewhere before and after the calculation. Early technologies were based on the magnetic polarization induced by electric current: rings of magnetic material were applied to a wired grid. If a low current was applied to a vertical and a horizontal wire, the ring at the intersection (and only there) was magnetized, and on observing the current during the begin of the operation, the stored value could be read out (Figure 2.2). Early versions of this storage were so heavy that before spending new memory to a computer often an architect had to be consulted, whether the floor was able to withstand the mass (the term "kilobyte" just had a physical meaning at that time).

Computers need programs. How to apply them to the computer? A keyboard to feed in code and data, and a printer to type out the results were also developed soon, but a program consisting of thousands of commands could not be retyped every time the program should run. One opportunity to feed code to the computer system was derived from a completely different engineering domain: mechanical musical instruments were already driven by punch cards since the end of the nineteenth century, and that technology was used for computers, too. The author can remember his time as postgraduate when he regularly carried a pile of about 6-7 feet of punch cards to the data center (Figure 2.3).

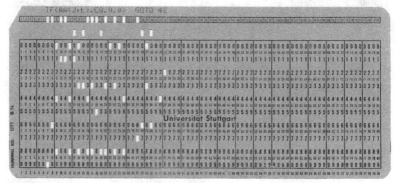

Figure 2.3: punch card with FORTRAN command line

Another technology was the usage of magnetic tapes already used to record speech or music. But enough of old techniques before we get into a discussion of stone hand axes, and back to modern electronics. To understand the following very basic physical knowledge like Ohm's law

$$U = R * I$$

will be sufficient. The rest will be done later in specialized courses.

2.2.2   Semiconductor Basics

From my own lectures at the university I know that the question *"what is a semiconductor?"* put to students in their first semester may get the answer *"well, take a conductor, and a very sharp knife ..."* Semiconductors seem to be seldom discussed during school time because a lot of teachers, or even my colleagues hold the opinion that basic technologies need not to be discussed if they are hidden so deeply in applications that it is not necessary to discuss them when explaining the application traits. Only specialists are inaugurated. I think this is a very short looking strategy. Even if the readers does not come into the situation to design an electronic circuit himself, it will be helpful to recognize a cock-and-bull story told by an impostor, and that's why i give a short introduction at his point.

Group→	1	2	3	4	5	6	7	8	9	10	11	12	13	14	15	16	17	18
↓Period																		
1	1 H																	2 He
2	3 Li	4 Be											5 B	6 C	7 N	8 O	9 F	10 Ne
3	11 Na	12 Mg											13 Al	14 Si	15 P	16 S	17 Cl	18 Ar
4	19 K	20 Ca	21 Sc	22 Ti	23 V	24 Cr	25 Mn	26 Fe	27 Co	28 Ni	29 Cu	30 Zn	31 Ga	32 Ge	33 As	34 Se	35 Br	36 Kr
5	37 Rb	38 Sr	39 Y	40 Zr	41 Nb	42 Mo	43 Tc	44 Ru	45 Rh	46 Pd	47 Ag	48 Cd	49 In	50 Sn	51 Sb	52 Te	53 I	54 Xe
6	55 Cs	56 Ba	*	72 Hf	73 Ta	74 W	75 Re	76 Os	77 Ir	78 Pt	79 Au	80 Hg	81 Tl	82 Pb	83 Bi	84 Po	85 At	86 Rn
7	87 Fr	88 Ra	**	104 Rf	105 Db	106 Sg	107 Bh	108 Hs	109 Mt	110 Ds	111 Rg	112 Cn	113 Uut	114 Fl	115 Uup	116 Lv	117 Uus	118 Uuo

		57 La	58 Ce	59 Pr	60 Nd	61 Pm	62 Sm	63 Eu	64 Gd	65 Tb	66 Dy	67 Ho	68 Er	69 Tm	70 Yb	71 Lu
*		89 Ac	90 Th	91 Pa	92 U	93 Np	94 Pu	95 Am	96 Cm	97 Bk	98 Cf	99 Es	100 Fm	101 Md	102 No	103 Lr
**																

Figure 2.4: periodic system of chemical elements

As the reader probably knows from chemistry, matter is composed of atoms, which have a dense nucleus, and electrons, which circle around the nucleus on well defined orbitals, each providing a well defined energy value for an electron in it. The electrons are distributed among the orbitals in a manner that at most only two electrons populate an orbital, and the energy sum of all electrons is at the minimum value. The number of electrons circling around the nucleus is a characteristic of each element. For Carbon, for instance, the number is 6, for Silicon 14, and so on, and the chemists have tabulated them in the periodic table of the elements according to the type of orbitals filled with the outer most electrons (Figure 2.4).

When atoms interact with each other and form chemical compounds, orbitals are formed that surround more than one nucleus, and if electrons populate these orbitals, a stable molecule or, on a larger scale, a solid or liquid body is formed (in compounds like salt the situation differs, but that is not interesting for our topic, and left out, therefore). Only the geometry changes, all other rules rest valid, and the chemists and physicists are able to determine which atomic orbitals transforms to which molecular orbitals.

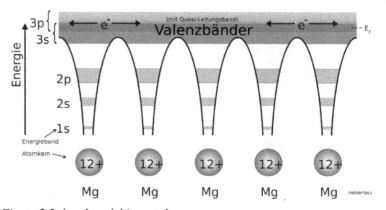

Figure 2.5: band model in metals

In solid bodies molecular orbitals covering merely the complete macroscopic body are build among other being well located at the nuclei. In metals the distributed orbitals, or valence bands are populated by electrons because the atomic orbitals which transform to valence bands are well filled in the atoms already. These electrons can, therefore, walk throughout the body. If an electric voltage is supplied to the body, the electrons leave the body at the positive contact, others enter is at the negative contact, and an electric current is flowing through the body (Figure 2.5).

In bodies of semiconductor materials like silicon, or in isolators, such distributed orbitals are also present, but they contain no electrons because the total number is too small to populate them. All electrons populate orbitals that are localized between the nuclei, and are therefore not able to move around, and for this reason pure semiconductors are primarily (weak) isolators.

The difference between semiconductors and pure isolators is that in semiconductors all localized orbitals up to the highest are completely filled, and the energy gap between the highest localized and the lowest distributed orbitals is rather small. Every additional electron will populate a distributed orbital, and therefore will enable the flow of electrical current.

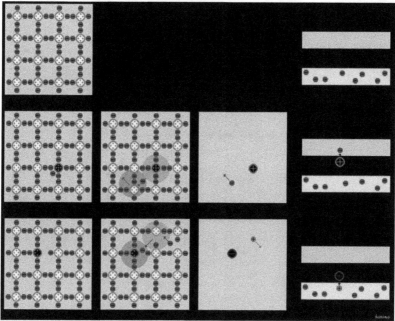

Figure 2.6: conduction mechanism in doped semiconductors

But semiconductors as pure silicon are still isolators, and to make them conductors we need a trick. The trick is to add small amounts of impurity to pure silicon. The impurity can be taken from both sides of the column of the periodic table silicon can be found in, for instance aluminum, or phosporus: aluminum has one electron less than silicon, phosphorus one additional electron. The effect of the impurities:

- If the silicon is "contaminated" with phosphorus atoms, these electrons will occupy distributed orbitals (mid row in Fehler: Referenz nicht gefunden, the N-layer in lower row), and the body will become a conductor because the additional electrons are able to move around.

- A contamination with aluminum will produces holes in the localized orbitals, which are also able to move through the crystal and conduct a current because the energy necessary to "steal" an electron from the neighbor is not very high, and the process will already happen at rather low temperatures (lower row in Fehler: Referenz nicht gefunden, the P-layer in Figure 2.7). Electrons will jump from gap to gap, but formally a positive charge is moving around.

Up to now this is not very exciting, but if we put both parts together, we get a component with completely new properties called "diode" (Figure 2.7):

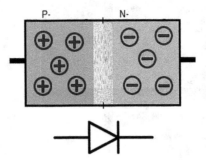

Figure 2.7: diode layers, and electronic symbol

At the border between the two parts, a transition zone is build where electrons in the distributed orbitals of the N layer may jump into a hole of the P layer. Because of the energy difference of the orbitals, the electrons do so for a certain extent, and an electrical potential difference results at an equilibrium point. Now we connect a battery voltage to both sides of the diode.

1. ⊕ P/N ⊖ : the jumping electrons in the P zone are pulled out of device leaving the positive holes without their counter parts. The electrons having passed the transition zone now fill the holes by jumping into the next free position until they eventually reach the contact, and are pulled out of the devices themselves.

The now missing electrons in the N layer from the transition process to the P layer are provided by the negative contact of the battery at the right.

A current is flowing.

2.   ⊖ **P/N** ⊕ : additional electrons are pulled into the holes of the P layer necessary to transport the electrons away from the transition layer by the battery, and the distributed orbitals of the N layer on the other side supplying the missing electrons in the first model are drained now. The transition layer now looks like a not doted pure semiconductor – an isolator.

No current is flowing.

A diode is, therefore, a switch letting pass an electric current only in one direction. Sure, we have to observe some boundary conditions: the diode is only a weak conductor or a weak isolator compared with real conductors or isolators. If the current in the conducting state gets to high, enough heat is produced due to the inner resistance of the diode to damage the device, and if the voltages gets in the isolating state gets to high, a current disrupts the transition layer damaging the devide too.

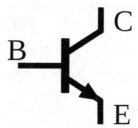

Figure 2.8: npn transistor

But the diode is not the end of the story, so we continue before coming to the application in our computer construction. If we combine two diodes, another new component is built: a transistor. A transistor is an enhanced diode construction but with three zones, either P-N-P or N-P-N, with the median zone being very thin. The N-P crossovers not just form a complete diode, but the dimensions remain in the order of the transition zone of a diode. This leads again to new, and surprising properties. The electric symbol for the new building block is presented in Figure 2.8.

Here, we discuss a transistor with npn layer sheme (the reader may well outline the corresponding pnp scheme himself). The + pole of the battery is now connected to C (collector), the − pole to E (emitter), and a small arbitrary voltage is supplied to B (base, Figure 2.8). The primary functionality can be deduced from the diode:

- If the base is supplied with no voltage, the diodes are in locked mode, and as the two N layers are separated by a diode forming layer, no current is flying at all.

- If the base is supplied with a positive voltage, the connection B → E is in conduct mode and a (very) small current is flowing (very small because the layer is very thin).

  The other connection B → C rests in locked mode (Figure 2.9), so no current is flowing on this side.

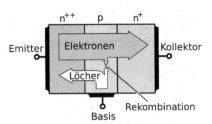

Figure 2.9: conduction mechanism

According to our understanding up to now nothing happens at the C connection. But in a measurement a current E → C will be measured, and it is much larger than the E → B current. So, where is the trick? The trick giving new properties is the very thin B layer and the very small connector at B. If it is thin and small enough, only a very small current is flowing through E → B, and most electrons recombining with the holes in the base layer are not captured by the base connection itself but travel into the empty electron band in C (drained by the positive voltage at C) leaving the holes back for capturing further electrons from E, and resulting in a large current E → C being directly proportional to the small control current E → B.

If the voltage at B is inverted, no control current is flowing from here to either other zone, because the holes in B which may be occupied by electrons from E have vanished, and C is already drained. This interrupts the current E → C, too: no current is flowing.

The main new feature is the proportionality of the currents E → B , and E → C. A transistor acts

- as a relay: a small control current can control a large operation current,

- as an amplifier: the higher the voltage at B (the resulting current can be neglected), the higher the current between E , and C.

Again some boundary conditions have to be observed to prevent damage from the component. These are only the very basics to understand the function of semiconductor parts. Varying materials, additives, and dimension allows the engineer to construct parts with very special properties.

Remark. If the reader visits lectures of physics, and electrical engineering during his studies, some confusion might appear. Physicians use the symbol i for the imaginary unit, and j for the electric current – the electrical engineers do it often just the other way round. For the physicians the direction of an electric current is the flow direction of the electrons $\ominus \to \oplus$, the electrical engineers let the current flow in the direction $\oplus \to \ominus$ as can be seen from the arrowheads in the diode, and transistor symbols. Don't be confused, just take it as folklore!

2.2.3   Simple logic circuits

It is very simple to construct the OR operation with only the two components resistor and diode using Ohm's law as can be seen from the following wiring diagram Figure 2.10.

The resistor is connected to 0 V, the inputs are arbitrary 0 V or +5 V. If the input is at zero level voltage, the relevant diode is in lock mode and no current is flowing. If at least one input has +5 V, the corresponding diode has a very low resistance, and according to Ohms law the output A is ~ +5 V because the whole voltage drop occurs at the resistor. If both inputs are zero, the resistor drags A to zero too re-gardless of the state before.

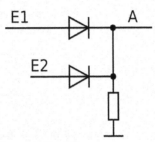

Figure 2.10: OR gate

The same principles allow the construction of the AND operation.

Exercise. Explain Figure 2.11 using the principles of the OR op-eration.

In this circuit, the resistor is terminated with +5 V instead of 0 V as in the preceding case, and the diodes are just lock in the other direc-tion.

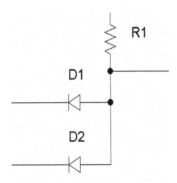

Figure 2.11: AND gate

It should be obvious that simple circuits like these two are not suffi-cient to build up a computer, even if we arrive at constructing a complete set (AND and OR are not complete, because at least NOT is missing). Circuits like these are passive with the effect that

- if the resistance value is high, the output current cannot become very high when the diodes lock. If the input resistance of the next circuit is similar to the resistor value itself, this will result in voltage break down. On the other hand,

- if the resistance value is small, a significant voltage loss at the output cannot be prevented when the diodes are open, and the inner resistance of the input device is similar to the resistance value.[1]

The effects are not so drastic if the resistance values are chosen carefully, but due to the resistor the + voltage loses some per cent of its value. The scalability requirement for our computer certainly results in large operator cascades, but after some steps a clear signal cannot be measured any more with passive devices due to this effect.

To save the situation, we turn the devices into active devices compensating the loss by using a transistor to make the inner resistance of the output lower than the inner resistance of the input. As we have proofed in our logic lesson, the NAND operator is a complete logical operator system, and, therefore, sufficient to do all kind of logic operations. A NAND gate is the destination of the following active device design.

We start with an AND gate composed of D1, D2, and R1 in Figure 2.12. The output of the passive AND circuit is connected via R3 to the base of a transistor Q1, which opens on a positive input voltage. Since the base needs only a very small current, the inner resistance of the input line may be rather high.

Q1 must be in conduction state when A and B are positive, and in locking state when at least one of the inputs A or B is negative. The serial resistor network R3/R4 should guarantee this. The resistor value of R4 only has to be rather high compared with R1, and R3 is only for adjustment of the transition levels of the transistor.

---

1   The input resistance can be calculated from a measurement of the current flowing through the device at desired voltage, the inner resistance can be measured by the current flowing through an electrical short.

If Q1 is in conducting state (the AND condition is true), the output Q is negative (NAND condition 1), and the inner resistance of the circuit is rather low. If R1 in the next circuit is rather high, the next logical level can easily be guaranteed to be definitely false.

If on the other hand Q1 is locked by one negative input, the output is high (NAND condition 2). Because the diodes in the next circuit lock, the resistor value of R2 is of lower importance. The correct response in the next circuit is guaranteed by R1/R3/R4.

Now we have done it. As we have concluded, the amplification step in NAND condition 1 allows for the construction of large operator cascades because the losses cannot sum up in a circuit line. Every circuit has only to deal with the next one, and hasn't to care about the total length of the circuit line.

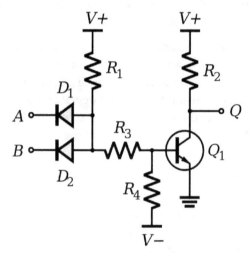

Figure 2.12: the universal NAND gate

The reader may feel it costly to design complex logics by only using a NAND. For certain also other active components like AND, OR, and XOR can be constructed directly without taking a detour by composing them of NAND circuits. In these cases further boundary conditions have to be fulfilled concerning the input and output resistor networks, but we leave the details to the engineers.

Another aspect we have not mentioned yet is the speed at which the circuits operate. If the diodes turn into lock mode, the resistors have to drive the voltage to the other level. Since the current is limited, the speed of voltage change depends on the capacity of the system. This has to be balanced too: if the resistance is too low, the states change very quick but the currents in open state are high producing heat which could damage the device.

2.3   Clock, and Memory Circuit

2.3.1   Towards Universality

Logical gates is not the only thing we need. Our computer shall be universal. To achieve the objective, we have to set up

- complex circuits doing all kinds of operations necessary and sufficient to execute arbitrary calculations (addition, multiplication, branching due to logical evaluations, and so on), and

- varying lists of serial execution commands of these circuits to execute a special calculation like evaluation of an integral, encryption of private data, and so on.

All complex circuits consist of a lot of NAND operations each, and it may be necessary to serialize some of these operations too, forinstance to implement an addition operation or something other.

To make clear the problem: serialization means that in the first step a set of input signals is processed for a short period of time until all output signals are available. When the operation step is done, the output signals are converted to input signals of other, or perhaps the same basic circuits, and again a short period of time has to be elapsed before the output → input conversion happens again.

Inner serialization can again be hardwired. For instance an addition operation acts on a lot of circuits in a chain, and there are no deviations from this working scheme regardless which values are added. So we can construct a complete circuit chain, activate the input voltages, wait for some time so that the signals at the output come to a stable and definitive state, and read out the output voltages. A multiplication of two numbers consists of repeated shift and addition operations, as we will see later on. Because multiplication is a standard operation, the effort of building a complex circuit to execute this operation is worthwhile, but it needs more time because of the multiple addition operations. Someone needs to keep count of what is happening to choose the appropriate working parameters. Perhaps the hardware engineer may feel it to be more efficient to implement addition and shift operations as basic circuits, and to reuse them multiple in multiplication. He must time each reuse carefully not to remix former results with new values then.

We haven't proven that inner serialization is inevitable, therefore, you could speculate that it may be possible to implement all circuits as monolithic blocks instead of being stingy, and reuse smaller parts again. But concerning outer serialization there is no way out. Each application comes along with its own series of circuit execution, and we cant even hardwire them, because that would violate the universality principle. The outer list must, therefore, be a "soft list", coded as electrical signals that control, which circuit is activated next. The conclusion is that we also need elements to store command signals, which would also give us the opportunity to store output signals that are not needed in the next operation step but later on.

2.3.2   The Clock

To deal with the serialization problem, a simple clock element – a multi vibrator – can be constructed from two transistors, and some other devices, now also including capacitors. A circuit of a simple multivibrator is shown in Figure 2.13.

How does this circuit work? The transistors are of npn type, so they need a positive voltage at the base to get conductive. When turning on the power supply, they are blocked. The voltage at the plates of the capacitors will now slowly grow because only small currents are flow-

ing through the resistors R1 - R4 . At some point eventually, the positive voltage at one transistor's base switches it into the conducting
state. Let us assume that Q2 enters the conducting state because
R1/R2 load C1 faster to the necessary positive potential. As effect
the ⊕ voltage pole of C2 drops suddenly to zero, and if the resistors
R3 and R4 are configured to produce a potential difference of, say, 0.7
V at the capacitor plates during the load process, the ⊖ plate of C2
drops to a negative voltage relative to the ground potential now locking Q1 definitely.

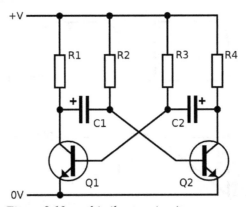

Figure 2.13: multi vibrator circuit

A small current flowing through R2 ensures that the base of Q2 remains on a positive voltage level and Q2, therefore, in the conducting
state. The current also ensures a small potential difference at the
plates of C1 which is important for the next cycle.

Meanwhile R3 slowly reloads the ⊖ plate of C2 to positive potential,
and at some point eventually Q1 becomes conducting. The potential
of the ⊕ plate of C1 drops to zero pulling the other pole to negative
values and locking Q2 immediately. As a consequence R4 pulls the
potential at the ⊕ plate of C2 to positive values, thus bringing the
other pole to even higher potentials which enforces the conducting
state of Q1.

Now the described circle starts again at R2 bringing Q2 to conducting state after a while and completing the cycle.

The switching between the two states is a sudden process because of the amplification traits of the transistors. The voltages at the points right and left of C1 are shown in Figure 2.14. At the outer point we can tap a rectangular signal – not quiet perfect but in good proximity. This can be used as a clock signal in logical circuits. At the inner point a sawtooth voltage is produced – not usable for us but perhaps for other purposes.

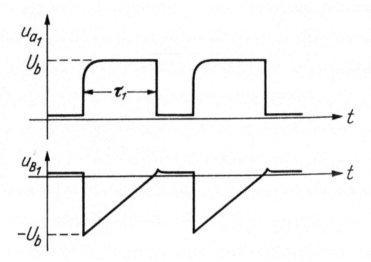

Figure 2.14: Voltage at left (upper) and right plate of C1

If the circuit is asymmetric (different resistance and capacitor values of the corresponding components) the signal can be varied from short pulses $0 \to U$ over regular rectangular output as in Figure 2.14 to short negative pulses $U \to 0$. Again, this circuit should only demonstrate that it is possible to reach the target. Circuits used in practice are far more sophisticated than in our example.

2.3.3   Memory Circuits

By means of a multi vibrator circuit, and a OR gate a simple memory device can be constructed:

a) If the vibrator is not provided with ⊕ voltage, the output of both capacitors is 0 V, which is equivalent to a stored zero.

b) If ⊕ voltage is supplied, at least one capacitor is in the ⊕ state. If both output lines at C1/C2 are connected to the input lines of a OR gate, a 1 could be read out constantly at the OR gate's output (and 0 in case a)).

If the output of the OR gate is fed back to the supply voltage input (an active OR gate would be preferable over the passive one presented in Figure 2.10), the memory state becomes persistent: once initiated with 0 or 1, the circuit remains in this state.

But to make this storage device usable we need further logics:

a) There will be multiple storage units. So we need a logic activating only one unit to deliver its state to the calculations circuits.

b) The same is true in the opposite direction. We need a logic activating only one unit to store a new state, and to do that exactly a the time point the value has become ready.

c) To store a value we have to overwrite the actual state forcing a $0 \to 0$, $0 \to 1$, $1 \to 1$, oder $1 \to 0$ transition.

To read out the state a AND gate, and a positive READ signal can be used. If the state should be read out, the READ signal rises to ⊕ voltage giving 0 or 1 at the output line depending on the state of the memory circuit. The outputs of many circuits can be connected by a OR^n gate with as many diodes as memory circuits.

When a signal is to be written to the memory, a WRITE signal has to be present. This is a little bit more tricky because there are 4 possible transistions (c). One solution is possible with two AND, one OR, and one NAND gate:

• The OR feed back gate is not directly connected to V+ of the vibrator circuit but trough a AND gate. The second input is the WRITE signal inverted by the NAND gate. Because the WRITE line is 0 when the device is not selected, the state of the OR feed back gate is readable as the output signal.

- If the WRITE signal changes to $\oplus$ voltage, the first AND gate is blocked to 0. The second AND gate combines the WRITE signal, and the value to be stored which is also displayed at the output.

- Both AND gates are connected by the OR gate now delivering either the stored state or the state to be store to the V+ connection of the multivibrator. If the WRITE signal is switched off, the state is preserved by the feed back circuit because all parts are designed as active circuits guaranteeing a stable power supply.

Again there exist other constructions for memory circuits in reality. This description should only give an impression for the newcomer how to proceed. The reader will surely perceive that timing conditions of the different parts will become very important when the system grows. For instance the multi vibrator and the OR gate in our memory circuit design must achieve a stable output state before switching the WRITE signal from high to low. To balance all is some kind of artwork.

Exercise. Try to construct a circuit design from the above and following description. The easiest way is to use boxes with their input lines at the left side, their outputs at the right, and their logic as text inside the box. Then only the appropriate inputs, and outputs have to be connected to each other, and the general I/O from outside.

2.3.4   Putting all together

Having discussed the design of the basic circuits, and some aspects how to connect them to bigger unit, we can now try to design more complex parts, and construct a computer. The most simple machine that we can build, will use the following requisites:

- A system clock delivering rectangular pulses.

- A counter (register) keeping count of the clock ticks.

- A set of hardwired complex circuits representing certain algorithms.

- Logic circuits to route the input signals to one of these algorithm circuits in dependence of special commands.

- Memory locations to store sequences of commands and data.

- Logics to address specific memory locations.

Only the clock, and the memory circuit are constructed in detail in this textbook up to here, some will follow because of their general importance. But most tasks will be left to special readings. The reader may try to outline the design of some simple circuits nevertheless to get a better understanding of the principles.

Exercise. Two signals can code the four addresses 00, 01, 10, and 11. Try to design a simple circuit with four output lines which have output 1 at one of the above combinations only.

This hardware design is coupled with a certain functional design. An algorithm consists of several commands how to proceed with the dealing of the data, and the commands have to be executed one after the other. Let us call the execution of one command a "machine cycle". The question how comprehensive one machine cycle will be in reality, will be answered later (and partly in other courses) because this depends on experience and analysis which commands are of basic type, and can be used to implement more complex types. The process is similar to the construction of complex hardware circuits from some basic circuits. A typical machine cycle, consisting of a multiple clock events, will be

1. Loading the command as a complete command line with supplemental informations from the memory location the clock counter points to to the command signal lines.

2. Loading the memory content which the command should handle, to the input signal lines. The memory address is the first supplemental information of the command.

3. Executing the algorithm another part of the command line specifies.

4. Storing the output of the algorithm to the memory which the last part of the command points to.

1. Loading the command .. .. ..

Although this model is much easier than today used models even on simple systems, the complexity of such a complete system is tremendous. But the reader should keep in mind that complexity is a relative concept. We have only had a look at the essential circuits, and what we call "*complex circuit consisting of essential circuits*", can be abstracted as circuits or chips as well, and the next abstraction layer will be constructed from chips and not from the basics.

For example: we constructed a memory cell for storing only one information bit using a WRITE, a SIGNAL, and an OUTPUT line. A command memory element, for example a byte, is constructed from several of those parts. It will be presented as a box with one WRITE, one SIGNAL, and n DATA lines. The single bit storage circuits and further logic circuits necessary will be hidden in the box, and it is again only one box in a bigger box containing many byte memory boxes and complex address logics to discriminate between them.

So it is possible to get to more and more complex structures without loosing the overall view. It is only a question of inserting an abstraction layer at the right position to get a new box, but if this principle comes out of sight, the situation gets desperate. "Only" is an understatement in this context however, because if the number of different boxes gets out of hand, the situation gets confusing too.

Some last additional aspects: though not absolutely necessary for our computer, a link to the analogue world would be desirable. Analogue values have to be transformed to digital values and vice versa. To get here, more complicated components would be needed like operational amplifiers, which contain 5-30 transistors depending on their quality and properties. The same will happen, if further devices as printers, displays, physical memory devices, or data transmission devices shall be connected to the machine. But that is far beyond the scope of our introductory textbook, therefore, we stop the hardware discussion here.

2.3.5   The Benefits

Not much imagination is needed to predict that even in optimized versions enormous amounts of these basic circuits are necessary to build up powerful computers. The early versions using electronic valves may fulfill our basic requirements in theory, but in practice the scalability will soon find a natural border, because the machines get to big, and heat producing, and/or consume too much time when the jobs get more demanding.

Figure 2.15: zone melting of silicon crystal

Semiconductor devices push out the practical limits far beyond. Electronic valves are manufactured from rather big metallic parts included in a vacuum glass bulb, and are dependent on a heating wire, which is the main source of the heat. Semiconductor devices don't need any heating and are much smaller from the beginning. And when techniques allow for faultless production, the devices don't need to be any longer single parts but can be arranged together in "super parts" or integrated circuits.

The secrets of miniaturization and faultless production are optical, chemical, and vapor chemical techniques, and of complex 3D circuit designs. The first step is the manufacturing of extremely pure semiconductor material. This can be achieved by zone melting: the already high purified material in rod shape is melted only in a thin layer, which then slowly migrates along the rod. Starting with a small mono crystal at the first melting point this results in

a)   a mono crystal of the semiconductor material with optimal properties for circuit construction, and

b)   the remaining of the last impurities in the liquid phase because of better solubility.

The pure crystal is cut in slices, on which the circuits are applied in a multi-step procedure. The production process is a sequence of the following steps (Figure 2.16):

a. Prepare wafer

b. Apply photoresist

c. Align photomask

d. Expose to UV light

e. Develop and remove photoresist exposed to UV light

f. Etch exposed oxide

g. Remove remaining photoresist

Figure 2.16: photo lithographic layer production

1. The surface of the so far produced incomplete IC or wafer is modified chemically, which can be done by

   a) exposing it to chemical reagents or

   b) steaming it with another surface layer from the vapor phase.

   The modification only concerns a new thin modified surface layer, not the entire wafer, or already applied circuits.

2. The surface is coated by a thin layer of photo resist.

3. The next layer design has been prepared as a photo mask, and the photo resist is exposed to UV light through the mask.

4. The development removes the photo resist where it was exposed to light, and the surface that was generated in step 1. is now open again to manipulation at these positions.

5. The part of the layer generated in 1. not covered by the photo resists is next removed by etching chemicals. The process must be designed in a way that the carrier layer below is not affected.

6. In the last step of the cycle the remains of the photo resist are removed. As a result, the primary sur-

face is now coated with the applied new material of step 1 only at the positions that the photo mask allows.

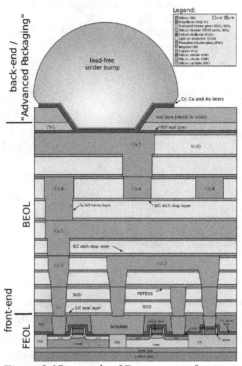

Figure 2.17: complex 3D structure of a CMOS device

These steps can now be repeated with some modifications until the complete integrated circuit it ready. Because different materials have to be applied as electrical active compounds (remember: a circuit consists of diodes, transistors, resistors, and capacitors, and all theses parts have to mounted to the wafer by this technique), wiring and perhaps shielding has also to be done, and at least there must be wiring connections to the outside. This leads to a rather complicated 3D design of the device (Figure 2.17).

In the course of time, the engineers changed the light exposure technique from normal photo techniques changed over uv light to X-ray techniques, thereby enabling minor structures (Figure 2.18).

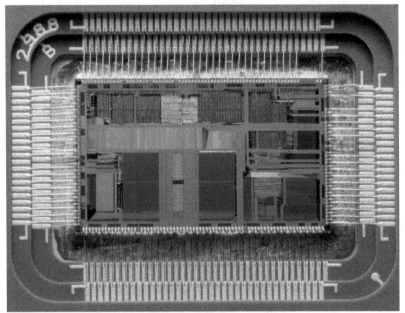

Figure 2.18: INTEL CPU chip of an outdated generation

As a result of miniaturization and the greater density of circuits on one wafer the hardware grew faster and faster, which gave theorists cause for the formulation of Moore's Law demanding that hardware speed doubles every 24 month. This prediction holds until today (Figure 2.19) although it describes an exponential growth, and due to this exponential growth a natural border of conventional techniques is in sight: when near atomic dimensions are achieved, the production process gets more error prone, and if only a few electrons are responsible for electrical effect, quantum effects and environmental influences may take over and cause errors in the results. Today other techniques take over to make programs run faster, and there are still unused techniques in the background. But that is another story.

The hardware speed has a draw back however, because

- software engineers care less about the efficiency of their technological part, and

- users demand the handling of very large data sets essential of which they didn't even know that such data exist, before one of the last generation of computers was able to produce a few of them with some effort.

Wirth's Law formulated in 1995 as a result of this bearings is as true as Moore's law, and lectures us:

"Software expands to fill the available memory."

"Software is getting slower more rapidly than hardware becomes faster."

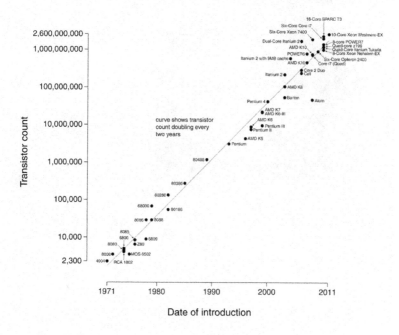

Figure 2.19: Moore's Law

3 Numbers

We have only been occupied with logics so far, but a computer shall calculate something. We as users, being convenient to do it ourselves, want to feed in numbers, and expect a numerical answer from the machine. This implies two challenges for the engineer:

a) How can a computer, only dealing with logics, be made to calculate numbers?

b) How trustworthy are the results?

It must by noted that most people, engineers often included, think that the job is done with realizing a). This is definitely not the case! Errors inherent in machine calculation often produce fatal results. The engineer has always to check whether a machine produced result is trustworthy (and that's why you should read this chapter carefully).

The phenomenon of trusting a computer unconditionally is more widespread than you perhaps think. Examples? Here they come:

- Some students may have made the unpleasant experience that they got a "fail" on presenting the results of mathematical exercises by simply copying them from a symbolic math program. Why? Well, the answer of the computer was correct, but didn't fit the question.

- The calculations results for the space telescope weren't checked before manufacturing, and the telescope didn't make its job (some parts of it were calculated the European metric system, others the British-American system). Another correction device had to be manufactured and brought into the earth's orbital by a space mission, and only God really know the cost.

- And in Germany the computer gave the maintenance team of a speed train an "OK, you have discovered a fail, but mount the part back, and tell nobody" after they hat detected a broken wheel. Result: 99 dead.

Reasons enough to deal in detail with this matter right from the beginning.

Insertion. Many flaws are based on a wrong conduct of students. Unfortunately school seldom teach the principles of good scientific practice because the teachers are too occupied with other problems. It is not quite simple to change a behavior adopted since adolescence when the proband passed the age of 20, but the universities should try, and explain. Here are some rules how to solve scientific tasks:

a) Every idea is valid at first. There is no law demanding a person has to produce the correct solution at the first onset, and nothing but the correct solution. You are not blundered if your first idea is wrong (instead, persons making someone ridiculus for a wrong idea in place of presenting a better idea blunder themselves). The first solution idea for 3*9 may be 30 forinstance. That is OK.

b) Every idea has to be tested carefully against know theorems. You can either try to prove that the idea is correct, or that the idea does not solve the problem.

This are different strategies: if you want to show the correctness of your answer, you don't doubt that the idea might be wrong, and you perhaps forget to ask important questions. In very complicated questions both strategies should be applied.

c) If the answer was incorrect, or the correctness cannot be shown, don't throw it away. It is part of the work, and should be represented along the correct solution as "paths that are excluded from delivering the correct solution".

Mind this definition! It is a positive definition. If the wrong path is documented, nobody would replay it, and loose time again. And in real life you will be fired if you present 100 code lines after 3 months work to your boss, because a lot of abortive paths had to be pursued. If you present another 2,000 code lines along with the proof that these paths cannot contribute to the success, you have shown that you really have worked the three months, and your boss will be impressed by your diligence.

These outer conduct should be supported by some inner conduct: often student only reflect on a exercise, but this is insufficient. All parts of your brain should be involved.

- Write down any idea on a paper sheet: the motoric parts of your brain are involved as well as the visual center, and the short-term memory buffer is relieved because you can remember all facts from the paper in parallel.

- Discuss it loud, and walk around, even if you are alone. Further parts of your brain are involved, and help you to find the solution.

- Discuss it publicly. This often lead on to more adrenaline production in your brain overclocking the normal work mode. I often experienced that students having a question, and being invited to present it at the blackboard, turn around after halve the way mumbling "a, ok, that's it", and sit down again.

- Stop working on the problem after some time. If the short-term memory of your brain is filled, it becomes very difficult to proceed. But this part of your brain becomes drained during sleep, and the "draining program" also keeps track of the importance of the facts stored, and transfers them to to long-term memory in a processed form. It will happen rather often that you wake up, and have the solution, or at least an important idea how to proceed.

3.1   Number Systems, and Integers

Our number system is something special because of the number, or better digit, zero. Of course other number systems also know of the number "nothing", but the trick is to use it as a digit to represent higher numbers. Ten is something like "one with nothing". This prin-ciple leads to a special representation which makes computing very easy.

We constrain our investigation firstly to integer numbers. Real num-bers come along with their own problems, and we be concerned with them in separate chapters. Every number can be represented by a set of digits and powers of a base:

$$1,335 = 1*10^3 + 3*10^2 + 3*10^1 + 5*10^0$$

Here, 10 is the base of the number system and $\{0,1,2,3,4,5,6,7,8,9\}$ or $\{z|0 \leq z \leq b-1\}$ are the digits. In practice, we can choose an arbi-trary base and the corresponding digit set:

$$B=7 \quad , \quad Z=\{0,1,2,,3,4,5,6\}$$

$$B=16 \quad , \quad Z=\{0,1,2,3,4,5,6,7,8,9,a,b,c,d,e,f\}$$

$$B=60 \quad , \quad Z=\{0,1,2,3,4,...,57,58,59\}$$

To some extend it is easy to deal with digits. Smaller bases, for exam-ple 8 – the octal number system – use less digits, and we only have to delete some digits – here 8 and 9 – from the list. For some higher sys-tems like the base 16 – the hexadecimal system – some characters of the alphabet are sufficient. But at least something like base 60 pro-duces some problems to find enough digit symbols, not even consid-ered the problem of clarity.

Computer hardware is naturally based on the base 2 (digits 0, and 1), and dealing with man, the hexadecimal oder perhaps the octal system will be used. But in virtual number systems on the computer, bases like 1,048,576 or higher may be used.

Back to the theory of number systems! How can a representation of a number in one system be transformed to a representation in another system? And exists always a representation of a number in another system? In practice:

$$1,456,999_{10} = ?_7$$

$$(58),(33)(17)(21)_{60} = ?_{10}$$

The solution is simple if we follow the above representation as a special polynomial (I assume that the reader is familiar with the concept of polynomials from math at school). Let us choose the base=10 system as a reference system, other systems as working systems (the definition of the reference system is, however, arbitrary). The calculation from a working system representation to the reference system is very easy because we need only to evaluate the powers of the base in the reference system multiplied with the corresponding digits, for example:

$$58*60^3+33*60^2+17*60^1+21*16^0=12,347,841_{10}$$

To develop an algorithm for the other direction, the same strategy may be applied: calculate the powers of the base, use them as divisors, ... That's OK and will result in the correct representation, but it's a tedious way. To make it more elegant (and to let the computer do the job eventually), we note down the polynomial form in slightly another way by recursively excluding the base from the sum term (perhaps the reader already knows of it, too):

$$\sum_{i=0}^{n} a_i*B^i=(..((a_n*B+a_{n-1})*B+a_{n-2})*...)*B+a_0$$

In this mathematical (sorry, engineering doesn't work without maths) formula I used the symbol Σ for a short representation of a sum. The sum symbol will be explained in detail in every math lesson, and the reader should become very familiar with it because in programming a sum is immediately transformed into a for-loop.

Exercise. Drill yourself to change from one polynomial representation to another without any problems. Write down the sum representation of

$$1-2*x+4*x^2-8*x^3+16*x^4-32*x^5+...$$

If the number 8,192 exists in this series, what is it's sign?

With the last representation, also known as Horner's representation, the transformation becomes easy. In the first step we arrive at:

$$1,443_{10}=206*7+1$$

We only have to do a division with remainder, and the remainder is the digit of 7^0 in out working representation. If we continue the division with remainder with the quotient of the preceding operation iteratively, we arrive at

$$1,443_{10} = 4,131_7$$

Thus as far as integer numbers are concerned we have developed algorithms to represent numbers in arbitrary systems, and from the algorithms it is clear that every number has a representation in every system.

To get from one working representation to another the reference representation may work as a relay.

Exercise. Calculate $4,325_6 = ?_9$

The calculation can be executed directly if one base is a multiple or power of another. The working base of a computer is 2, but this small base results in very long representations of even small numbers. The representations get shorter if $8 = 2^3$ or $16 = 2^4$ is used. Here we only need to convert the digit of base 8 or base 16 to the digit representation of base 2 and concatenate the representations, or to convert a group of digits of base 2 to a digit of the other bases.

Exercise. Calculate $2A_{16} = ?_2$, $73_8 = ?_2$, $A33_{16} = ?_8$
$1101001101011001010_2 = ?_8 = ?_{16}$

Remark. This introduction may be very short compared with the effort often spent in lectures where often several boards are filled with complete example calculations. I propose another way: if you think to have understood the calculation principle implement it in Java or C or whatsoever programming language is taught in a parallel course and let the computer do the tedious calculations. If it works you have won!

Exercise. Another way to make use of a computer to execute the tedious parts of the computations is to utilize a table document application like MS Excel or LibreOffice Calc. Most readers will be familiar with these programs from school.

Implement table sheets doing the different conversions. The recursions/iterations can be done in sequent lines.

3.2 Calculations

From the polynomial representation of a number we can also easily derive algorithms for addition and multiplication. Math tells us (important! Visit the math lessons to get familiar with this!)

$$\left(\sum_{i=0}^{n} a_i * x^i\right) + \left(\sum_{i=0}^{n} b_i * x^i\right) = \sum_{i=0}^{n} (a_i + b_i) * x^i$$

$$\left(\sum_{i=0}^{n} a_i * x^i\right) * \left(\sum_{k=0}^{n} b_k * x^k\right) = \sum_{i=0}^{n} \sum_{k=0}^{n} (a_i * b_k) * x^{i+k}$$

For the beginner, this may be confusing, but if you have a further look at it, adding to numbers in polynomial notation is nothing else than what we learned at the elementary school with only one additional operation:

$$7*10^2 + 4*10^1 + 5*10^0 +$$
$$1*10^2 + 9*10^1 + 6*10^0 =$$
$$8*10^2 + 13*10^1 + 11*10^0 =$$
$$9*10^2 + 4*10^1 + 1*10^0$$

The digits at the corresponding powers are added. If the sum is greater than the base, only the remainder is retained and the quotient is added to the next higher power. This is executed until all digits are less than the base. The only thing that has to be added to polynomial addition to obtain a number addition, is the iterative reduction of the digit starting at the most right side: divide the sum by the base and note only the remainder instead of the sum while adding the quotient to the next higher base potential.

> **Exercise.** As the reader should be familiar with this scheme since his time at elementary school, write down the multiplication scheme for 125 * 568 in the same manor.

Subtraction is as easy as addition, but we have to take care of the sign:

```
 1   7   3   -
 6   3   5   =
-5   4  -2   =
-4  -6  -2
```

At first glance some readers may be confused. How to achieve -462 from the polynomial subtraction intermediate -5 +4 -2 ? Again this is nothing else than the application of the basic rules learned in the elementary school. Since electronic calculators are introduced very early in school today, the pupils have a lot of time to forget even basic rules, but you will certainly remember after a while. The complete rules for addition/subtraction are:

1. Calculate pre-digits by adding or subtracting the digits at corresponding powers of the base

2. Look at the digit of the highest power. If it is positive, the whole number is positive, if it is negative, the number is negative, regardless of the signs of the other digits

> **Exercise.** Justify this theorem using the polynomial representation with powers of the base. The sum of all lower powers cannot exceed the value of the highest digit, even if the highest digit is a "1", all others being "9".

3. If the number is positive:

    Start at the right most position, that is the digit at $base^0$. Do the following steps recursively for all digits until you reach the left most position.

    a) If the digit ist positive:

If the pre-digit is bigger than the base, subtract the base, and add a 1 to the next higher pre-digit. Repeat this until the digit is less than the base-

b) If the digit is negative:

Add the base, and subtract a 1 from the next position. Repeat this until the digit is greater or equal zero.

After recursion all digits are positive and less than the base.

4. If the number is negative:

Again start at the right most position, and repeat until you reach the left most position.

a) If the digit is positive:

Subtract the base, and add a 1 to the next higher pre-digit. Repeat this until the digit is negative.

b) If the digit is negative:

If the digit is less than the negative value of the base, add the base, and subtract a 1 from the next position. Repeat this until the digit is greater than the negative value of the base.

After recursion, all digits are negative (or zero), and bigger than the negative of the base.

In the last step of these operations it may be necessary to extend or shorten the number representation because the highest digit is greater than the base, or becomes zero.

Exercise. Again it may be helpful to teach a computer to do this job. If you are already experience in programming, you may try to implement these rules in a Java, or C++ program. Instead of repeated addition, or subtraction you should use quotient, and remainder of a division. Readers with less experience in programming may try to realize the rules in a table calculation application.

The rules may become a little more complicated if we add or subtract several numbers at a time before digit correction, but it can always be broken down to a simple scheme that is easy to implement as a software algorithm. Such algorithm implementation are inevitable, if the task is to deal with big numbers which appear in cryptography like (this really is one number!)

```
BC 51 A3 D8 69 F1 3D 32 C6 E3 20 F8 0F A5 F3 38
6B A6 8A F1 72 6D 63 AF 4C D1 E7 6F AF 1F C5 47
E5 8A B2 60 19 B3 EB C9 62 6F 57 36 94 9D E1 FD
51 36 5F 91 53 04 A1 BE 17 88 CA A7 9D A0 51 EF
AF AE 77 74 4A AA EC 62 A9 5C 28 1A 3D D9 81 C1
63 F3 62 A7 78 A9 F5 1D 16 B2 0C AC 4B 39 D8 D2
02 65 25 F7 7E B4 AB 5B D9 DC 21 EA D1 18 6A 38
E0 42 3D 6A 0D 98 6F 3A 65 BA FA FA 69 C3 63 FD
A1 AD EC 93 1A 7B 28 C7 33 29 AB E3 66 C3 0D D5
76 52 FD 24 9A 8A A1 31 05 7A 4C 0B A4 8C B3 94
71 48 3C A5 70 E9 BE 56 78 44 80 6A 41 4A E7 A9
7E 17 1B F2 64 CA 8B 95 9A 63 B7 68 16 62 FC 42
B8 A2 56 28 8F 54 F8 65 96 F5 E1 C3 78 68 9F 33
92 26 7C 43 28 9D BC C8 9D AB 33 D9 33 1A E4 5D
5A E4 1B D9 23 02 DB 5F 53 5E 64 15 F0 55 21 FE
11 0B 0C A2 B8 72 94 FC 9C FA B7 1F 8F 75 55
39_16
```

The only algorithm being more complicated is the division. There are two possibilities depending on the base. In both descriptions we assume that the numbers are positive. Since the sign convention is easy and well known, we can always make the numbers positive before the calculation, and correct the sign of the result after having finished:

1. The shift/subtract method:

    a) Shift the divisor left as much as possible so that the result of a subtraction remains positive. "Shift left" means that the digits are transferred to the next higher power of the base, and a zero is written to the lowest power. Count the number of shifts you have done.

    b) Subtract the shifted number from the dividend as long as the result remains positive. The count of possible subtractions is written to the digit of the result at the shift position count.

    For example: to calculate 744:43, the first step is

$$744-(43*10)=314 \quad \Rightarrow \quad quot=1\mathrm{x}$$

c) Now shift the divisor to the right until positive subtraction is possible again, and repeat with step b)

$$314-(7*43)=13 \quad \Rightarrow \quad quot=17$$

The shift right is the inverse operation of the shift left, and the zeros added at lower powers of the base are lost again.

If no further right shift is possible because we got the original divisor again, the result register contains the quotient, the the former dividend now is the remainder.

2. The digit conversion/division method:

a) concatenate the last two digits of the dividend and divide it by the highest digit of the divisor. Note the quotient in the result variable at the power of the base which is the difference of the powers of the dividend, and divisor base powers.

For example, to calculate 121:33, the first step is

$$1*10^2+2*10^1+3*10^0:3*10^1+3*10^0 \rightarrow$$
$$12*10^1+3*10^0:3*10^1+3*10^0 \rightarrow$$
$$12*10^1:3*10^1=4*10^0$$

Note the quotient also in a fresh temporary variable.

b) Multiply the divisor with the temporary variable, and subtract the product from the dividend

$$1*10^2+2*10^1+1*10^0-(4*10^0*(3*10^1+3*10^0))$$
$$=-1*10^1-1*10^0$$

As the example demonstrates, negative results are possible in this operation. The negative intermediate may be obtained, followed by a sign correction at the end of the algorithm, or the divisor is added to the dividend, and a "1" is subtracted from the last result digit.

c) Repeat this operation until the dividend is less than the divisor. Again, the result variable contains the quotient, the dividend the remainder.

Remark. The concatenation at the beginning guarantees that the result of the division is greater than zero. If the digit of the dividend is already greater than that of the divisor, the concatenation may be omitted. This rule is important for the last step, because the dividend may be still greater than the divisor, but the powers are equal, and a concatenation is not possible therefore, because this would result in negative exponents.

The advantage of the second method: if addition, subtraction, and multiplication for polynomials is implemented, the division can be implemented using these operators, whereas the shift/subtract method has to be implemented from scratch.

> **Exercise.** Calculate some examples of division with both methods and figure out how sign correction has to be carried out.
>
> Again try to use a computer (programming language, or table calculation) to do the job. The description of the algorithm is quite extensive but contains some tricky details you can only learn from an implementation exercise.

The mathematical reason for the complicated algorithm of division is that integer numbers and polynomials obey the same algebraic laws if and only if the polynomial coefficients are members of a field that is at least rational numbers. But we only can deal with integer digits here which form only a ring.[2] In a ring the remainder of polynomial division may have the degree (the highest power) of the dividend, whereas in a field the degree is less than that of the divisor, as is the case for integer division.

In case of addition and multiplication the ring property of the polynomial coefficients is of no interest because rationals cannot appear. Fortunately the situation can be won even for the division if we take into account the digit correction schemes.

---

2   In a mathematical field a quotient without remainder is defined for all elements except zero as divisor, whereas in a ring most elements can only be divided by others leaving a remainder.

> **Exercise.** Show in detail that the degree of the dividend is at least reduced by one, and a valid quotient digit not equal zero results if the highest digit is concatenated with the second highest.
>
> Remark: the degree of the dividend must be greater than the degree of the divisor. If the degree of the dividend is reduced by more than one, a zero quotient digit is produced.

3.3   Binary Calculations in Practice

Binary calculations are as easy realized as in the previous chapter in other bases:

```
    1  0  1  1  0  0  1  +
    1  1  0  0  1  1  1  =
   10  1  1  1  1  1 10  =
 1  1  0  0  0  0  0  0

 1  0  1  1  *  1  0  1  =
 1  0  1  1  +
    0  0  0  0  +
       1  0  1  1  =
 1  1  0  0  1  1
```

On a paper sheet a multiplication may be done in one step, which requires the addition of up to n intermediate results if the number has n bits (=digits; we will use bits in the further discussion if we deal with binary numbers; we will also shorten the formulations to "bit at position n" for the bit at the power 2^n).

> **Exercise.** In practice the multiplication is done gradually by shift operations, and bit checking of the divisor. If k-th bit of one factor is set in the k-th shift operation, the shifted second value is added to the result.
>
> Develop an algorithm for the multiplication using
>
> IF (conditional operation) bifurcation, if the right most bit of one factor is set (AND 1 operation),

ADD operation to add the first factor to the result (initialized with zero) when the condition tested by the subsequent IF is true,

SHL (shift left one bit position of the complete number loosing the highest bit in each step and filling with zero bit from the left),

```
SHL 11001101 = 10011010
```

for the first factor which was conditionally added,

SHR (the same for the other shift direction)for the second factor to move the next higher bit to the right most position.

Continue until all bits are processed. Verify that the result must have twice the number of bits of the factors if the multiplication should have a valid result in every case. Derive a rule for multiplication operation with all numbers having the same length n. If the highest bit set to 1 in factor 1 is at position k, which is the highest position for a bit set to 1 in factor 2 in order to produce a valid result?

How to realize that on our hypothetical computer? We have so far only developed logical circuits. So let us have a look at an arbitrary digit. We have to **add** the digits of both numbers and (!) the transfer of the calculation before, the so called "carry bit". Possible states are

Bit 1	Bit 2	Carry	Result	Next Carry
0	0	0	0	0
0	0	1	1	0
1	0	0	1	0
0	1	0	1	0
1	1	0	0	1
1	0	1	0	1
0	1	1	0	1
1	1	1	1	1

Exercise. If you write down the logics for the result and the new carry using AND, OR, and NOT, you will get some lengthy terms. Do this!

Exercise. The rules are slightly different for a subtraction because now 0-1 produces a carry bit. Construct a table for this operation.

As these terms even get more lengthy if you transfer them to use only the NAND circuit, it may be adequate to think about other special circuits being more slim, for example

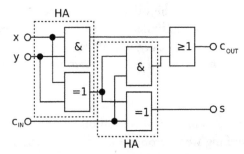

Figure 3.1: adder logic

which uses two AND (&), two XOR (=1), and one OR (≥1) circuits, or this one

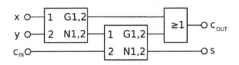

Figure 3.2: another adder logic

using two halve adders and a XOR operation. Using adder circuits, and a shift operation we can realize the multiplication as you already learned from the exercise. If the addition is extended to three input bits, and the carry bit, the shift operation can be saved by direct wiring. In this multiply addition the bits of the factors are AND connected, and the result is added along with the carry bit to the result bit. To carry out one step of the multiplication, only one bit of factor

2 is involved, but all bits of the other values. The shift operation is done virtually in each step. Because only ADD is used in the n steps, this hard wiring is faster than a software solution also implementing SHL and SHR.

Exercise. Try to construct a direct multiplication circuit for two numbers of three bits (remember: the result also occupies three bits; three is a nasty number in reality, but big enough for an exercise).

As can be observed the addition of two numbers can end with a carry if at least the highest bit of one number is set and a carry bit propagates to this position or the other number also contains a 1 in the highest position. In a multiplication the number of bits is formally doubled each time. Statistically, therefore, only the lower half of the bits of the factors may contain a 1, with compensation of bigger numbers by smaller ones possible (see derived rule in one of the above exercises).

A carry bit after a complete operation on all bits, therefore, tells the user that something went wrong. A so called overflow happened. For technical calculations it should be reflected in advance how big the numbers can grow during calculation, and an appropriate number of bits for representation has to be selected.

To put it on a computer hardware, we must decide how many digits or bits have to be used as standards. The engineers decided to implement the following bit numbers for number representations in hardware design and programming languages:

Name	No. of Bits	Range
Byte	8	256
Word	16	65,536
Double word	32	4,294,967,296
Quad word	64	9.223.372.036.854.775.808

Beyond this we have to use software algorithms to represent numbers, and execute calculations (see "big number" in the last chapter).

The next question which we have to deal with: how to represent negative numbers? Do we need a special sign bit? This may be one strategy, and we did so in the discussion of the theory of numbers, but this complicates out circuits, again and there is a more simple possibility visible if we subtract 1 from 0 :

```
0 0 0 0 0 0 0 -
0 0 0 0 0 0 1 =
1 1 1 1 1 1 1
```

If the last carry of the operation is simply discarded, the remaining number 1 1 1 1 1 1 1 is the representation for -1_{10} ! Or as a general rule: if the highest bit of a number representation is set, the number is implicit negative, and to invert a number you have simply to build the two complement according to

```
- (a7 93 bf c8) =
  a7 93 bf c8 ^ ff ff ff ff + 1 =
  58 6c 40 38
```

This can easily be derived from the construction of the number -1. If all bits of 1 are inverted (XOR with a complete FF mask is an inversion. Prove this!), the result is 1 1 1 1 1 1 1 0, and we have to add one to produce -1. You can prove this with arbitrary numbers subtracting a large positive number from a smaller one.

In the last example the start number is negative, the resulting number is positive again, and we see that

$$a7\ 93\ bf\ c8_{16,16} = -1,483,489,336_{10}$$

In this example we have used the hexadecimal notation instead of the binary notation. Larger series of binary digits become unmanageable, but 4 digits ranging from 0 0 0 0 to 1 1 1 1 can directly be mapped to the digits 0 .. F of the hexadecimal system which is only ¼ of the length of the binary representation. ^ is the XOR operation we mentioned earlier, which has the outcome 0 if both inputs are 0 or 1, and 1 otherwise.

Exercise. Verify with arbitrary calculations that a subtraction can be replaced by a two complement of the number to be subtracted, and a normal addition of the negative number.

In further exercises you can easily prove, the there is (nearly) no need to take care of the sign of a number. If the numbers are in the range of the number of bits used, the result will be correct anyhow. The advantages of the two complement are:

- We need not to take care of the sign of a number, but can just add (or subtract) them regardsless whether they a positive or negative.

- Subtraction can done by building the two complement of a number, and an ordinary addition instead of constructing special circuits for subtraction.

- Multiplication can be done directly. In the overflow rule for the multiplication of positive numbers the 0s in the upper positions have only be substituted by 1. You can easily verify this as an **exercise** by calculating the two complement of the negative numbers, executing the well known multiplication with positive numbers, and building the two complement again.

- Division can also be implemented by help of the two complement in the known way.

- To print out the value of a negative number, just build the two complement, print out the positive value, and put a "-" before. All rules to change between number systems can thus be maintained.

Exercise. If numbers are interpreted as signed numbers, the overflow bit doesn't indicate an error. An overflow bit can occur even when correct result is produced. An error is now indicated by a wrong sign bit. For instance an addition of two positive numbers can result in a negative number (why does no overflow occur in this case?). Create a complete set of rules for the detection of invalid results, each rule provided with an example.

We leave it to you to show:

Exercise. Division can be done by shifting operations, and subtraction (see exercise in the last chapter beginning with the maximal possible left shift of the divisor).

A subtraction should only be carried out if the result is positive, and a 1 is placed in the corresponding position of the result in this case. Instead of executing a subtraction followed by an addition if the result is negative, try to construct a bit comparison scheme for the GREATER operator ($>$) of two (positive) numbers.

At the end of this chapter you may have had the disturbing feeling that I left a lot to exercises instead of explaining it in depth. But all here is simple stuff based on elementary school principles. You can easily derive examples with known results and compare them to your trials. If something doesn't fit, you can alter your algorithm until you found the mistake. All that results in a deep comprehension of the matter, and the experimental work is at least daily routine of an engineer.

Remark. The question remains whether numbers on a computer are interpreted as unsigned numbers with a greater range, or as signed numbers. Perhaps the reader may think that signed numbers are more important than unsigned numbers, and therefore the implementation is restricted to signed numbers.

The engineers were less rigorous, and left the decision to the programmers who can either use INT oder UNSIGNED INT as data types. The discrimination between signed, and unsigned numbers is mostly done in the programming language. The CPU discriminates between signed, and unsigned only in essential cases, for instance in a division where special assembler commands are involved:

```
unsigned int i1,i2,i3;
i1=i2/i3;

0x40141a    mov     eax,DWORD PTR [rbp-0x48]
0x40141d    mov     edx,0x0
0x401422    div     DWORD PTR [rbp-0x44]
0x401425    mov     DWORD PTR [rbp-0x40],eax

unsigned int i1,i2,i3;
i1=i2/i3;
```

```
0x401428    mov     eax,DWORD PTR [rbp-0x3c]
0x40142b    cdq
0x40142c    idiv    DWORD PTR [rbp-0x38]
0x40142f    mov     DWORD PTR [rbp-0x34],eax
```

It is the job of the programmer to use the appropriate type. For instance the code

```
unsigned int i;
for(i=15;i>=0;i--)
```

results in a loop that never stops (why?).

There are a lot of rules to identify a result as being invalid, as you have derived in one of the exercises. The computer, however, doesn't react on an invalid outcome of an operation, but continues to run the program to its normal end, and delivers some nasty results.[3] The reason behind this philosophy: calculations with integral numbers are absolutely exact, so the programmer has to take care to declare appropriate data types in advance which are able store the results correctly in every case. If he doesn't care he has probably chosen the wrong job.

3.4   Real Numbers

3.4.1   The Principles

Calculations using integer numbers can in principal be constructed in a style that the result is exact, but in most areas of daily life we operate on fractional numbers. Principally it should be possible to maintain exact calculations if we use rational representations (fractions

---

3   This is not always true of coarse, because it is sometimes difficult to decide which type is appropriate in a certain situation. Most systems offer a debug mode for this purpose which produces a message on an invalid outcome. But this verifications cost time, and should be disabled before the application is delivered to the customer. We come back to this in chapter 4.

a/*b*), and avoid things like roots, logarithms, and so on which cannot be represented by a finite number, or fraction. But counters and denominators get quickly unmanageable large after some calculations even if the number is reduced by the greatest common divisor of counter and denominator. Inaccuracies are unavoidable, and the best known method to approach the correct value is to make use of terminated continued fraction, but this is so awkward that teacher avoid such topics at school.

In practice rationals are, therefore, real numbers are transformed to floating point numbers, for example

$$1/4 = 0.25$$

Unfortunately most of the rationals don't transform in this simple way but have a periodical fractional representation like   1/3 . It may be possible to maintain with some tricks even then exact results, but you will have to evaluate digit intervals in length of the lowest common multiple of the periods of both numbers, which becomes unmanageable, too. In a lot of calculations it is impossible too to discard irrational numbers like roots, or transcendental numbers like π, and from both reasons we are accustomed to cut the number of digits after a while, for example:

$$1/3 = 0.33333333 \quad , \quad 2/3 = 0.66666667$$

The exact result is rounded up or down to the nearest representation value, with dramatical effects, because

$$1/3 + 1/3 \simeq 0.66666666 \quad \neq \quad 2/3 = 0.66666667$$

We will occupy with this phenomenon later on. But note the difference between integer and real numbers on calculators:

- Integers are cut in the highest terms of the polynomial representation whereas

- real numbers are cut in the lowest!

The fractional representation in combination with rounding can now be applied to binary numbers. A REAL binary number is represented by the (inverse) polynomial term

$$r = \left(\sum_{k=1}^{n} a_k 2^{-k} \right) * 2^e$$

Instead of positive powers of the base the polynomial term is build of negative powers. Formally this progression doesn't stop at a specific negative power, as we have seen. We have to define ourselves, how many digits should be kept for almost every real number.

To guarantee that each number is stored with the same precision, another trick is used right from the beginning. The representation only contains summands of negative powers of the base which are adjusted by an additional term with a positive power. One possibility of representation is to fix the decimal point to a specific position, and reserve a fixed number of integer, and fractional digits:

$$xxxxxx.fffff$$

We could for instance reserve 32 digits for the whole number in this way, but what about a number like

$$r = 0.0000000006546578745 \quad ?$$

Most of the existing digits are cut away for storing the leading zeros.[4] To store the number at the highest possible precision (in non zero digits), the number is shifted to $r' = 0.6546578745$, and the shifting exponent is stored in a separate register. In each number stored in this way:

- all stored digits – the **mantissa** – are valid and the first digit will always be non zero,

- the magnitude of the number is adjusted by an **exponent**.

---

4   In then programming language COBOL exactly this way of representing numbers was chosen. COBOL was developed for economic calculations, not for scientific calculations. The distribution of an amount of money to several parties can always be done in an unambiguous way by such calculations because the problem discussed with $1/3 + 1/3$ does not occur.

3.4.2   Base Transformations

First of all we have again to develop algorithms to change the bases. Having a binary number, and wanting a floating point number is a trivial job as we can use the same algorithms as before.

Exercise. Develop an algorithm to transform real numbers from the working base to the reference base. The algorithm should follow Horner's Scheme.

But what is about the other way round, changing from our reference base to a working base? A number in our reference base may have the representation

$$10.359 = 1*10^1 + 0*10^0 + 3*10^{-1} + 5*10^{-2} + 9*10^{-3}$$
$$0.000725 = 0*10^{-1} + .. + 7*10^{-4} + 2*10^{-5} + 5*10^{-6}$$

If we don't change these representations we

- have to mix integer number calculations arising from the part left to the decimal point of the first number with fraction number calculations of the right part, which cannot be a very good idea if all algorithms should remain simple,

- and loose precision in the second number because of the inverse power series.

The first step is to normalize the numbers to "scientific notation"

$$0.10359*10^2 \quad \text{or} \quad 0.725*10^{-3}$$

Now, only fraction number calculation algorithms have to be applied, and full precision is guaranteed. But we can't do it in a simple way! As easily can be seen, there is no way to represent 10^2 by a power of 2, because $2^6=64$, and $2^7=128$. So we don't have to divide, or multiply by 10 until the normalized representation is achieved but to divide, or multiply by 2:

$$10.359 = 0.6474375 * 2^4$$

The end of the normalization is a fractional number $0.5 \leq r < 1$. This yields the first part of the transformation algorithm:

```
while(Number > 1)
```

```
            divide by 2
            add 1 to exponent

        while(Number < 0.5)
            multipliy by 2;
            subtract 1 from exponent
```

As a result we now have numbers of the form[5]

```
    0.axxxxxx with 9 ≥ a ≥ 5
```

and can look for another algorithm to do the transformation

$$0.543 = 5*1/10 + 4*(1/10)^2 + 3*(1/10)^3$$
$$= (a_1*1/2 + a_2*1/4 + a_3*1/8 + ...)*2^e$$

First observation: most fractional numbers in the base 10 having only a few digits will have a periodic presentation in binary notation. The reason is very simple. According to the addition theorem of rational numbers the equation

$$\frac{a_1}{(2*5)} + \frac{a_2}{(2*2*5*5)} + ... = \frac{b_1}{2} + \frac{b_2}{(2+2)} + ...$$

can only have a solution when all coefficients a_k are multiples of powers of the number 5 in the remainders and, therefore, the prime factor 5 vanishes in all terms on the left side. If this is not the case, the series on the right side will be infinite but periodical.

The conclusion of this observation: if we want to identify the exact period to execute a precise rounding operation, it is necessary to calculate the counters of the terms on the right side faultless, which means that we have to calculate them using only integers and not floating point numbers!

On rearranging the power series in Horner's manner, we arrive after some short reflexions at the following algorithm:

1. Multiply the number by 2

    Example $(r = 0.545)*2 = 1.090$

---

5   It is not mandatory to cut down numbers greater 1, but this leads to more complicated algorithms.

2. If the resulting number is bigger than 1, we note a 1 in the corresponding position our binary representation, and return only with the fractional part to step 1.

    Example: $f = 0.1$, $r = 0.090$

3. If the number is less than 1, we note a 0 for the binary bit and return to step 1 without any further change

    Example: $2*0.090 = 0.180$, $f = 0.10$

If you continue this algorithm, you will observe that every step is exact, and the fraction can be calculated at arbitrary length. We only need integers with as many digits as the fractional number has in total at the beginning. There is no need of big numbers for the calculation of the fractional part in arbitrary length.

> **Exercise.** I stopped here because the period length is longer than this. If you already had a programming lesson, try to develop a short program transforming the values, and determining the length of the period.

Attention! If you do so, don't use the data type DOUBLE to do the calculation! By entering a number into a DOUBLE variable all calculations you shall perform is already done, and the value is truncated internally. Therefore, it is impossible to get the right result. You must use INT variables!

This exercise can again also be done using a table calculation program like Excel for those among the readers not being familiar with a programming language.

3.4.3   Calculations with Real Numbers

As a further difference to integer numbers except the separately from the mantissa stored exponent the floating point numbers need a special bit to store the sign. The first bit – at the same time the highest bit in the polynomial representation – is always 1, hence the mechanism used in integer presentation is not possible.

This has consequences for addition and subtraction:

- The signs of the numbers have to be evaluated whether the operation is a true addition or a true subtraction. For instance $(-a)+(+b)=-(b-a)$, $(-a)+(-b)=-(a+b)$, and so on, a,b being unsigned numbers in this notation.

- In case of a true subtraction the bigger number has to be taken as the first operand, $b>a$: $a-b=-(b-a)$.

Exercise. Alternatively calculations can be done using the two complement again. Thereto the mantissa is interpreted as a signed integer number, the sign bit is used to perform a conditional two complement, the calculation is done as was explained in the integer number section, and if the result is a negative number, the sign bit is set, and the number two complemented. Develop an algorithm scheme, and prove it by doing some example calculations.

To perform calculations with floating point numbers nothing has to be changed for a multiplication algorithm except addition of the exponents and XORing the sign bits.

Exercise. Develop a complete multiplication algorithm using integer multiplication and addition. Explain how rounding is done.

Very important! To perform additions, or subtractions the numbers have to be transformed to the same exponent:

$$0.4456*10^0+0.3422*10^2=0.0044*10^2+0.3422*10^2=0.3467*10^2$$

I build the example in the reference system, but it is the same in the binary system. This has far reaching consequences: because the number of digits is limited – at least the result has the same number of digits as the summands – this normalization to the same exponent is barely different from a SHR operation erasing digits of the smaller number, and resulting in further errors which add to the errors already present from the base transformations. In floating point number calculation 4/5 rounding is done to minimize the error, but an error is present nevertheless. We wil deal with this in detail in the next paragraph.

> **Exercise.** Develop a complete addition/subtraction algorithm using integer addition/subtraction. Explain how rounding is done and the sign is computed.

The rest of the mechanics of floating point numbers should be clear. Like integer numbers floating point numbers are standardized, the most common representations being

	IEEE 754	
	Mantisse (in Bit)	Exponent (in Bit)
Single	23	8
Double	52	11
Extended	nicht exakt definiert	

Figure 3.3: standard floating point formats

The most used floating point format on a computer is **double**. Each double value contains about 16 decimal mantissa digits, the exponent can vary in the range of ±300.

In practice most floating point calculations are done on a specialized CPU which gives chance to some further tricks in the representations.

Remark. The first bit of the mantissa of a floating point number is 1, so it needs not to be stored, and one bit is gained. The number

```
1.000010101...
```

is stored on a DOUBLE as

```
000010101...
```

If you have experienced pointer operations in a programming language like C/C++ already, you can print out the bit pattern of a

DOUBLE by using an INT pointer pointing to the same address. This is an interesting experiment giving practical inside to theory. Victims of JAVA have unfortunately bad luck.

3.5   Errors, and Error Propagation

Calculating with real numbers is a devil's factory. If the same calculation is done on INTEL, MOTOROLA or IBM CPUs the results must not coincide! This is often not noticed because not all 16 digits of a double are presented in the result, or the human eye fails to see that because 16 is far larger than the 5-8 things our brain can manage simultaneously. But if you concentrate on a comparison of all digits, differences in the last 2-4 digits can be noticed.

Howdy! Aren't the engineers able to do their work properly? Of course they did proper work, but they didn't agree on the construction principles. Some manufactures calculate with doubles as defined in Figure 3.3, but others as the Intel engineers decided to calculate internally with 80 bit floats instead of 64 bit doubles. If this minor change in philosophy already results in differences, a shorter examination of the whole problem is in the order of the day.

3.5.1   Sources of Errors

Nearly every floating point number includes an error as we have noticed. The first error occurs when we note rational numbers or irrational numbers as fractional numbers in decimal notation due to rounding, the next error during conversion to binary floats due to another rounding necessary because of the incompatibility of the prime factor composition of the bases. The error is small however – the 15th or 16th digit – but can we ignore this?

In practice even after rather long calculations the result is exact up to 12-14 digits most cases which may be a sufficient precision. Do we have to check for this, or should we simply trust the result? If we don't trust our computation, we can repeat the calculation using 128 bit floats (or even longer). Sometimes this may be not appropriate, since even today machines are in use that cost some 10,000 $ per hour calculation time, and you will here some unpleasant comments from your boss if you want him to spend some other 10,000 $ for a new computation. On the other hand, if someone constructs a bridge of say 2,000 feet length, and at the end there remains a gap of 2 feet, really nobody will be very happy with this situation except some lawyers. So it's better to work in some systematics.

It is not very hard to see that computation is a devil's factory. From math we are used to some very basic laws: associativity, distributivity, and commutativity.

$$A + (B + C) = (A + B) + C$$
$$A * (B + C) = A * B + A * C$$
$$A + B = B + A$$

Nothing of that is true on a computer, although the violation of commutativity is a little bit hard to proof.

Exercise. Proof the violations of the first two laws yourself. Take some number varying in the exponents and observe the last digits which are not the same in different runs if you choose them carefully.

Of course the effects of such simple trials are very small again. But in the journal "Scientific American" an example of solving only two equations for two unknown variables was presented where in the result only the first digit was correct – the rest was waste. So there must be more.

To bring in some systematic we note the exact values with capital letters (X,Y,..), the actual values are noted in lower case (x,y,...). Then

$$\Delta = X - x$$

is the absolute error, and

$$\delta = \frac{X - x}{X}$$

the relative error. In practice an error range is often provided like
15.5±0.4. Here the maximum of the absolute error is 0.4, a value
with no real sense without reference to 15.5; the maximum relative
error is 0.0258 or 2.58% which can be dealt with without a reference.

From the last term we also derive $x = X(1 \pm \delta)$. If we add two values, which means a real addition or an addition of two positive values
respectively a subtraction of two negative values, we get

$$x + y = X(1 + \delta_x) + Y(1 + \delta_y) = (X + Y) + (X * \delta_x + Y * \delta_y)$$

or if we divide by $(X + Y)$, and change over to unsigned values to
describe the worst possible case

$$|\delta_{x+y}| \le \left|\frac{X}{X+Y}\right| * |\delta_x| + \left|\frac{Y}{X+Y}\right| * |\delta_y|$$

In the worst case the resulting error of an addition is in the same order as the largest input error, or

$$|\delta_{new}| \approx |\delta_{old}|$$

if $|X| \approx |Y| \wedge |\delta_x| \approx |\delta_y|$. Hence addition is uncritical even in longer
calculations.

The calculation is however incorrect in one respect: the resulting error doesn't take into account the rounding at the end of the operation
concerning the last bit. To be correct we must write

$$|\delta_{x+y}| \le .... + \epsilon$$

ϵ being the elementary rounding error. This error doesn't play an important role in one calculation, but can sum up in longer calculation
chains.

Please remember: this is the worst case possible! If we use this formula to predict the accuracy at the end of a longer calculation we will
probably arrive at less then 3 valid digits. Experience tells us that in
most calculations most digits are precise however. This is due to statistical reasons. In a great number of calculations an error in positive
direction is compensated by an error in negative direction, either in a
simple calculation step as the above addition ($\delta_x < 0 \wedge \delta_y > 0$), or in
steps following each other. Hence errors of size 10^{-15} seldom sum up
above size 10^{-13} even in millions of operations.

Is that the end of the road? Should we stop our investigations at this point? It is seldom a good advice to resume "it'll be OK" from an intermediate result. Let's continue the road to the end:

Doing the same operation on a multiplication we arrive directly at

$$x*y = X*Y*(1+\delta_x+\delta_y)$$

Here we have neglected the term $\delta_x*\delta_y$ because δ is assumed as small value, and the square of a small value is a vanishing small value which is of no importance in the sum therefore. Changing to unsigned values to evaluate the worst case again, we see

$$|\delta_{x*y}| \le |\delta_x|+|\delta_y|+\epsilon$$

The error of the multiplication result is about double times the input value in worst case, hence multiplication is uncritical too.

Execise. Using the same systematics it is possible to show that the same is true for a division: it behaves like the multiplication. Try to show that.

Remark: it's a little bit tricky to move the error term from the remainder to the counter. You have to use the binomial formula

$$(a+b)*(a-b)=a^2-b^2$$

The rest was explained in the multiplication evaluation.

The critical moment arrives in the last investigation, a real subtraction, which means that the unsigned value of the result is less then at least the unsigned biggest input value. Here we get

$$|\delta_{x+y}| \le \left|\frac{X}{X-Y}\right|*|\delta_x|+\left|\frac{Y}{X-Y}\right|*|\delta_y|$$

If $X \approx Y$ then $X-Y \approx 0$, and the fractions become very large, and logically the resulting error may be some powers of ten bigger than the input values! A real subtraction may be absolutely critical in longer calculations.

The reason for this can be seen easily by watching the evolution of the mantissa. For example

```
0.123456 | 5655   -
0.123455 | 3433 =
0.000001 | 2222 =
0.100000 * 10⁻⁵
```

In this example the numbers stored on the computer are cut after 6 digits, the digits after | representing the exact values. But the exact values are not present; the stored numbers end at position |, the further digits of the numbers are assumed to be zero. Instead of the exact result 0.12222 only 0.1 is calculated which differs from the exact result by 22%, whereas the errors of the operands are about 0.004%.

We have done these investigations for one calculation step but longer computations consist of a chain of calculation steps for each resulting value. If we carry out sophisticated mathematical investigations using calculus on complete algorithms, it can be shown that alone the rounding error ε contained in the last bit can result in totally unusable results.

Exercise (only for programmers with some experience). Tchebycheff polynomials are recursively defined by

$$T_0(x)=1 \; , \; T_1(x)=x \; , \; T_n(x)=2*x*T_{n-1}(x)-T_{n-2}(x)$$

This harmless definition has some serious impacts. Implementations using the data type **float** (32 Bit) show no common digit with implementations using the data type **double** (64 bit) even at rather small values of n. Even the sign may differ.

The problem with all that: we don't know whether this burst of errors will happen during an arbitrary calculation. So we should take some measure against it, if possible.

3.5.2 Controlling Errors

In most theoretical considerations the worst case is determined, meaning that all small errors add up in the same direction to a large error. But statistically the errors of different steps can wipe out each other, as we pointed out already, and the result is better than the assessment. Often it is impossible to guess even the worst case error because the intermediate values of an algorithm are unknown. Do subtractions of similar numbers resulting in large errors appear, or not? Is the final result large compared to the flawed values which make them unimportant, or is the final result a value near zero? If the programmer doesn't know, he can try to get an assessment of the errors from the calculation itself. There are several methods which can be used in dependence of the algorithm:

- Positive and negative values can be added separately in two partial sums. If the partial sums are almost equal, the result must be viewed with more caution (this method should only be used for controlling because the final result is worse in most cases than the one achieved by normal calculation).

- The maximum subtotal can be observed. If it is big compared with the result, more parts of the calculation work flow are not submitted to extinction errors of leading bits.

- The calculation can be repeated with other mantissa length. We had proposed that already.

- The calculation can be carried out as an interval calculation to produce three values as result:

  ○ the normal operation value with 4/5 rounding operation,

  ○ the minimum result with rounding each value in the calculation to the nearest smaller number, and

  ○ the maximum result with rounding each value to the nearest larger number.

  This calculation method is complicated because the "nearest smaller/larger number" is not as easy to be determined as the concept signalizes, and is only useful on special hardware because each calculation has to be performed three times. The evaluation of the result and the result range is complicated, too.

3.5.3 Controlling Algorithms

It is possible to avoid a critical subtraction in an algorithm if it is definitely known that a subtraction will appear. Have for instance a look at the solution of a quadratic equation:

$$x^2 + p * x + q = 0 \quad \Rightarrow \quad x_{1,2} = \frac{-p}{2} \pm \sqrt{\left(\frac{p}{2}\right)^2 - q}$$

The subtraction under the root is not avoidable but the subtraction before the root is. If $p \gg q$ and we use the formula to determine both values, then $(p/2)^2 - q \approx (p/2)^2$, and hence $x_1 = p$, $x_2 = 0$. But only the first value will pass a test, the second not because the outcome will be $q = 0$ which is untrue even in the rounded computer world (think of using the values in further calculations: distinctive cases will probably produce completely false results).

To find a solution we take into account that the term on the left side of the quadratic equation is a polynomial of degree 2, and a polynomial with algebraic roots also has a representation as a product of root terms. Using the equality

$$x^2 + p * x + q = (x - x_1) * (x - x_2)$$

will give the solution

$$x_2 = q / x_1$$

for the second root which will produce correct results in a test and hence further calculations.

Such methods are called "numerical stabilization". Of course the stabilized form will only be necessary if one root is near zero. But a stabilized implementation is "state of the art" for a computer scientist, and you should occupy with this in technical programming.

4 Programming and Complexity

4.1 Our Computer Model

In the preceding chapters we were occupied by the question how to make calculations possible. That there will be more to do was only noticed at the edge. Let us at first develop a complete model.

From the logic principles we have developed, complex electronic circuits can be constructed taking input from at least two data entries of for instance 32 bit and producing an output of 32 bit. Let us call these data ports "registers" of the processing unit containing the algorithm circuits.

Which algorithm has to be taken next is determined by a command word. We reserve another 32 bit register for commands, which guaranties that we have enough savings for a large number of different commands. The 0s and 1s of a command activate one calculating algorithm and lock the others by some logic circuits.

One single command is not enough to do universal complex things. To solve a certain job several commands have to be put in a chain, and to execute them the input and output registers have to be reloaded or saved. For this purpose we provide special memory devices containing 32 bit values each. The memory devices are wired with our processing unit by a 32 bit bus system, the "data bus". Each memory position has to be clearly addressable, which is again done by a bit 32 bus system, the "address bus". As the reader may perhaps remember we need a special READ/WRITE wire to tell the memory device whether it should deliver or store a value on the data bus.

The data addresses are part of the commands, or more precise, a command tells the processing unit that it shall store the output register in the memory specified by a 32 bit address following the command itself or load an input value in the same manor. Input values can also be loaded directly, or more precisely, the command tells the processing unit to load a constant value specified by the next 32 bit in the command chain. To handle all this over the bus system – commands and data can be stored in the same kind of memory devices and use the same bus systems – further 32 bit registers for address operations are necessary. They are loaded via the data bus, and the values appear on the address bus in the next read or write operation for input and output registers.

Last not least we implement a clock delivering rectangular signals, each signal inducing the load of the next command, the next address, initiating the next algorithm, or the next transfer to storage – again some sophisticated circuit logic depending on the step before. Because the commands have to be taken from a memory device as well, we need a special register, the program counter, which tells us where to find the next command or address.

That's it. Lets resume:

- Registers in the processing unit:
    - two or more data registers for input and output,
    - one or more registers for memory addresses,
    - a program counter.
- Logical circuits:
    - algorithm circuits,
    - loading circuits for memory addresses from the bus,
    - exchanging circuits for transferring data over the bus,
    - loading circuits for commands over the bus.
- A bus systems for commands, addresses, data, and transfer direction of data
- One or more addressable memory device for data and program.
- A clock device activating the next program step on each cycle.

Okay, a lot of stuff, but in sum only assiduity work. In practice, modern processing units (CPUs) contain much more registers (Figure 4.1) because dealing with software technology introduces further aspects like special purpose registers, indirect addressing, and more.

Intel 80386 registers			
3_1 ...	1_5 ... 0_7 ...		0_0 (bit position)
Main registers (8/16/32 bits)			
EAX	AX	AL	A register
EBX	BX	BL	B register
ECX	CX	CL	C register
EDX	DX	DL	D register
Index registers (16/32 bits)			
ESI	SI		Source Index
EDI	DI		Destination Index
EBP	BP		Base Pointer
ESP	SP		Stack Pointer
Program counter (16/32 bits)			
EIP	IP		Instruction Pointer
Segment selectors (16 bits)			
	CS		Code Segment
	DS		Data Segment
	ES		ExtraSegment
	FS		F Segment
	GS		G Segment
	SS		Stack Segment

Status register

1_7 1_6 1_5 1_4 1_3 1_2 1_1 1_0 0_9 0_8 0_7 0_6 0_5 0_4 0_3 0_2 0_1 0_0 (bit position)

V	R	0	N	IOPL	O	D	I	T	S	Z	0	A	0	P	1	C	EFlags

Figure 4.1: register set of an elder INTEL CPU

The inner construction of a processing unit grows accordingly. Figure 4.2 Presents an overview of the CPU architecture of the same CPU. The reader probably doesn't understand all the details of this architecture, but it gives a good impression of the complexity that we circumscribed with "some further logical circuits" here.

Besides the CPU, the memory, and the bus system many more devices appear in modern computers, starting for instance with a spe-

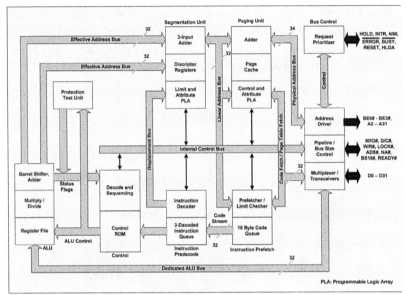

Figure 4.2: CPU architecture of INTEL 80386

cial CPU for floating point calculation, graphics, and so on. We will refer to some of them in later chapters.

4.2   Programming as a new Language

4.2.1   Avoid Confusion

Though being technical impressive the computer is only a piece of metal and plastics, and to do some work we have to tell him what to do, meaning that we have to write a program. A program or application has to contain all details of the calculation, and the computer is not able to do things we couldn't do ourselves. If we don't know how to do certain things, or if we are not able to express the necessary commands, the computer can't do it either.

A beginner's programming course may be a little bit confusing. If you want to hit a nail into a wall, your father may have told you " *take the nail in the left hand between thumb and forefinger, then take the hammer on the right hand but at the end of the handle, ...*" - a very detailed explanation what to do, including the advice to sprint to the next water crane to cool your thumb if it was hit by the hammer.

In a programming course it can happen that a professor is hovering into the room to herald that "*all the world is composed of objects, and it are objects that interact, ...*" -, and a person without a handyman as father would perhaps be so confused to take a saw to do the job of the hammer. Results of an object oriented programming philosophy starting to early.

We start here with a procedural method which is exactly what your father told you about hammer and nail. If the program gets very sophisticated and large, pure procedural method become error prone, and to prevent the programmer from making errors, therefore, some programming tricks are introduced into the programming languages. If the programmer uses them, the language interpreter will stop him on errors before a fault result is produced on the customer's computer, an event only pleasing lawyers. The result of these error avoiding mechanisms in the programming language is called object oriented programming, and you may get there without ever using the confusing object philosophy.

Keyword "programming language": you really have to learn a new language, whether it is C, C++, Java, FORTRAN, Lisp, Smalltalk, COBOL, C#, D++, JavaScript, PHP, Prolog, or whatsoever. If you analyze how to express a sentence in another language you will surely observe that you begin by forming the sentence in your native language, then translating it to the target language, and perhaps modify the native sentence if you are not able to produce a correct translation. For the first steps in programming it may be helpful to skip the translation and phrase the program only in native language. We will restrict ourselves to this part and leave the translation to the programming course.

4.2.2   The Way of Thinking

To formulate a program that a computer can work with is more complicated than obvious because we tend to omit trivial steps in a command sequence, or just jump over some commands of which we don't
know exactly which one we should take. As an example a text is to examined whether it contains a certain key word, and when found the
word is to be exchanged by another one:

```
lirum, larum, löffelstiel, wer das nict kann, der
kann nict viel

exchange: nict → nicht
```

The first shot of a beginner often sounds like that:

1.   Read the text until you reach the word "nict"

2.   Wipe it out

3.   Insert "nicht" instead

4.   Continue to the end of the text

Surely that doesn't work. If you compare the command with the construction details of the computer, the global command "read a word
of arbitrary length" is not implemented. You must explain to the computer how to read a text. Also the condition "until you reach the word
..." is not implemented. We only have registers of a limited length, so
how to decide whether an arbitrary word is reached? The same applies to "wipe out" and "insert". But the biggest nut is the command
"continue to the end". Continue what? Consuming electricity? No,
we have to be much more precise.

Before continuing I suppose an experimental section to a group of
readers. Our computer model can be mapped to some paper sheets
on which the state of the operation is noted after each step. Now
choose one of your companions to read aloud the next command, a
second one to execute the command on the paper sheets, and a third
one who is sent outside the room and the door shut. The experiment
whether your program is executable on a computer is very simple: execute an arbitrary amount of commands, then make a break and ask
your external coworker to come in. If the door was shut and he had

no connections to the NSA, he really doesn't know exactly what has happened so far. Now the next command is read out, and the candidate has to execute it on the paper sheets. If this works on every trial then your "program" is OK, but if

- your colleague looks around clueless or

- his head begins to smoke because he is trying to find out how to continue, or

- an error occurs,

you have left out some fundamental details and should re-engineer your process.

Now to the details. The first problem to solve is to decide how to organize the data, and how to use the memory. To store a sentence in a way to access words or characters we can use a checkered paper sheet. Each cell contains only one character, and through the index of the cells we can access a character without any doubt. To identify the end of the sentence we can place there a special character that doesn't appear in ordinary texts, for example, the character '#'. For our mission we need at least three such paper sheets named "sentence", "search", and "exchange" which are filled with the specific character sequences. This is the input, and we don't care about who supplies this input.

During our operations we need to note down where we are just doing something in the character sequences. For this we need paper sheets with numbers on it, and we name them like "pos_sentence" and so on so that we can identify which index belongs to which character sequence. How many of these sheets we need might not be clear in the beginning, and if we forgot one, we have to re-engineer out process. But that's a normal incident.

After having organized the data we can begin with the algorithm. The first step is

1. Initialization

    a) Get the input sheets

    b) Note a 1 on "pos_sentence"

If further sheet with numbers are needed, they also should be initial-ized to certain values, but you can re-engineer this step later. "Get the input sheets" may also be specified further depending on the cus-tomer supplying these sheets. Perhaps he will give you the original sheets, but don't want them to be changed, and you will have to make a copy for the work. But we don't care about such details now.

Out computer construction allows for the comparison of two charac-ters at a time, not more. To start our algorithm we can search for the occurrence of the first character of the search sequence in the sen-tence. We make use of our index sheet:

2. Search for first character

    a) if the character in "sentence" indexed by "pos_sentence" matches the character in "search" at position 1 then con-tinue at step 3.

    b) change the value on "pos_sentence" adding 1

    c) if the character in "sentence" indexed by "pos_sentence" is not equal to the character '#' then continue at step 2.a)

    d) return "sentence" to the customer

Some beginners might begin a program like: "compare at position 1, ... compare at position 2, ... compare at position 3, ..." It es easy to see that the program will get very long and even doesn't solve the problem if we foresee sentences of a maximum length of 2,000 char-acters, and the customer supplies Tolstoi's "War and Peace". The loops, as they are called, in our program version returning the control to a position that ends in the decision step again do that in a more el-egant and always working way.

As you will have recognized, part 2 of our algorithm already includes the end of the operation. If the end character is found, the result is re-turned and we can drink a beer as reward for doing a good job.

If the first character of search is found, we continue at step 3. Here we must check whether the other characters also fit, but we must care not to loose "pos_sentence".

3. Check rest of search sentence

    a) Initialize "pos_check" with value 1

b) if the character in "sentence" indexed by the sum of "pos_sentence" and "pos_check" does not match the character in "search" indexed by "pos_check" + 1 then goto 2.a)

c) change the value on "pos_check" by adding 1

d) if the character in "search" at position "pos_check"+1 equals character '#' then goto step 4

The command sequence returns to the search sequence if both character sequences don't match, and continues with the next step if they do. A detailed analysis of 3. will show that there might be unexpected results. If the search sentence is only one character long, the end is not found because the first end check happens on index three. These are typical errors in programming which have to be detected during testing (see below).

4. Wipe out operation

a) re-initialize "pos_check" with value 1

b) Initialize "pos_wipe" with value 0

c) exchange the character with index "pos_sentence" + "pos_wipe" by character "pos_sentence" + "pos_wipe" +1 in "sentence"

d) if the character at "pos_sentence" + "pos_wipe" in "sentence" does match '#' then goto step 4.f)

e) add 1 to "pos_wipe" and goto step 4.c)

f) add 1 to "pos_check"

g) if the character at pos "pos_check" in "search" does not match '#',then goto step 4.b)

h) goto step 5

Well that's a little bit hard because the usage of the index counters is a little bit tricky. If you tried it by yourself, you might have got another command chain using perhaps more index variables. But the operation itself should be clear: for each character in "search" all following characters in "sentence" move down one position, and in the end the whole search sequence is wiped out.

Exercise. Step 5 now inserts the value "change" in "sentence". This is done by inverting the wipe out operation: for each character of "change" all following characters of "sentence" are moved up one position before inserting the new character. Complete the program and check it by the proposed method.

At the end of the whole operation the easiest way is to jump back to 2.b). This may in practice also cause some errors if the search sentence is part of the exchange sentence.

I have already indicated that the program contains a lot of bugs which you might find during your exercises. Re-engineer your program accordingly. We come back to this some time later.

4.2.3   Concepts of Programming Languages

After finishing basic programming exercises in human daily language you change to doing the same thing in computer language which means that the detailed command list has to be structured and translated.

The most basic programming language is assembler which directly uses the machine code that we referred to in the starting paragraph of this chapter. Typical assembler code might look like this

```
org 100h
start:
    mov dx,meldung1
    mov ah,9h
    int 021h
    mov ah, 01h   ; read keyboard
    int 021h
    cmp al, '5'

    ja 11
    mov dx,meldung2
    mov ah,9h
    int 021h
    jmp ende
```

```
11: mov dx,meldung3
    mov ah,9h
    int 021h
ende:
    mov ah,4Ch
    int 21h

section .data
meldung1: db 'enter number:', 13, 10, '$'
meldung2: db 13, 10, 'number <= 5', 13, 10, '$'
meldung3: db 13, 10, 'number > 5' , 13, 10, '$'
```

We can identify our proposals of chapter 4.1 as well as the basic programming technique in the example code. Commands consist of a
command word plus optional constants or addresses, and depending
on the logic the control is transferred to the next command line or to
a specified line at another address. Out paper sheets appear as well as
specified memory addresses filled with constants or with results during the computation.

As the reader may have recognized already, assembler programs are
hard to maintain, or even to code when the application gets more
complicated. You can see directly what's happening in the CPU but
you don't get an image what it is good for. Therefore, direct assembler
programming is only used for very basic purposes. Most applications
are programmed using "high level" languages, and one of the most
basic is the programming language C which was primarily developed
for the programming of operating systems. A program in C may look
like this (it is just not pure C but contains C++ elements):

```
int main(int argc, char **argv) {
  cout << "prozess-user/group"
       << getuid() << " " << getgid() << endl;
  if(argc<2) exit(1);
  if(argc>=3){
    if(setgid(lexical_cast<uid_t>(argv[2]))!=0){
      cout << "errno=" << errno << endl;
      exit(1);
  }
  }
  .. ..
  args = (char**) malloc(20 * sizeof(char**));
  memset(args,0,20 * sizeof(char**));
  for(int i=3;i<argc;i++)
```

```
    args[i-3]=argv[i];
   execv(argv[3],args);
   return 1;
}
```

The picture has changed to the opposite: you can directly deduce what should be done by the code, but you cannot see how the CPU really executes this in detail. The former procedural concept is maintained, but new concepts are introduced:

- A command line can take more than one text line, commands are closed with ";".

- Complexer commands comprising multiple assembler command line are defined.

- Commands can be grouped by brackets.

- Decisions can be made by "if .. then .. else .." constructs instead of "jmp", which is far easier to control by the programmer.

- Loops like "for" do the same job as "if .. goto .." when repetition is necessary.

- A function concept with definition of local variables (memory addresses) and interface variables is introduced which make proper re-usage of code simple.

- Several different types of variable are defined, and the usage is directly controlled by the language translator.

We don't go into further details because that is the job of a programming course. If you look at the two code examples, you probably may understand why I started with a programming lesson in human language. Thinking directly in C will be easier in the end, but it may be more difficult to achieve the detailed thinking in a start up.

All high level languages provide their own translator which tells the machine in assembler what to do. Some are interpretor languages, some compiler languages, the difference being:

- **Interpretor:** the commands are evaluated at run time, and the interpretor calls machine code (in principle assembler

code which has been transferred from text to *n* bit values)
command line by command line.

- **Compiler:** the commands are first translated to assembler
  code and the ready machine code is directly executed. This
  method is far faster than interpretor code.

The next step are object oriented languages like C++ or Java. Often
code and data are not separable, and it is wiser to encapsulate them
so that other parts of a program cannot access forbidden data and do
harm to the result. The encapsulations are called "classes":

```
class DBase {
private:
  DBase();
  DBase(DBase const&);

  mysqlpp::Connection conn;
  string serv;

public:
  static DBase& obj(){
    static DBase o;
    return o;
  }

  void connect(string server, string user,
               string passwd, string base);
  bool bad();
  void delete_file(int fnr,string);
  ...
};
```

The concept brings along language terms like "private", "public",
"constructor", and others. Again this is not the place to explain that
in detail, and again this kind of programming leads to some new way
of thinking about application design. Starting from scratch as we did
this way of thinking develops automatically, but starting directly with
objects often is confusing.

Further concepts of classes are

- Inheritance: a new class can proceed on an existing one with
  specialized operations, for instance

  ```
  class Honda: public Car { ...
  ```

The specialized "Honda" cars use the properties owned by all cars and defines only the special additional properties of Honda cars.

- Operator and function overloading: methods up to operators (C++ only) can be redefined, and the correct code is selected by the compiler depending on the class object

```
A& opertor+=(A const&)
```

- Templates and meta programming: techniques ranging fom simple models to very abstract algorithms on data types

```
template <typename T1, typename T2>
struct Typelist {
  T1 first;
  T2 second;
};//end struct
```

Because of the large variety and concepts of languages the logical next question is:

4.2.4   Which Language is the best?

If you look through some web pages, you might find people proclaiming "*this or that programming language is the only one to use, all others being children's junk*". Thinking a little bit pragmatic this opinion is junk itself.

A handyman will use the best suited tool for a job, and so should do the programmer. A company would ask three questions to decide which tool to take:

1.   How long does it take to learn the handling of a certain tool?

2.   How long does it take for the tool to complete the job?

3.   How many jobs are to be executed?

Let us look at an example to clarify this:

Job: Programming a Web Browser	
Tool: C++ language	Tool: Lisp language
Learning Phase: 0 months	Learning Phase: 4 months
Production: 8 months	Production: 6 months
Similar Jobs: 0 – use C++	
Similar Jobs: 1 - use C++	or use Lisp
	Similar Jobs: 2 – use Lisp

If only one job of that kind is to execute, the programming team will loose two months on changing to another technology. Two jobs of that kind and the situation is balanced, three or more jobs will be profitable on using the other technology. The only thing remaining: the first job will take two additionally month to completion when the technology is changed, the profit coming with the new jobs. That might perhaps the CEO force to take another decision.

We will not go further into the details of the different languages and their suitability for a certain task because there are a lot of aspects to be evaluated. But at least you should justify your decision to use a certain technology with a little more than "it's the best language whatsoever". Software technology as an advanced course will teach you the measurements to be taken.

In terms of education however the question becomes another weight. Even if some colleagues are not very enthusiastic about such statements, I would prefer C/C++ for educational purposes. The two main benefits would be

- C/C++ forces the programmer to care about a lot of things that are absent in other languages (because it is implicitly done by the system itself instead of the programmer).

    C/C++ is, therefore, downgrade compatible meaning that a C/C++ programmer wouldn't make any errors when he implements a program in Java because he only has to forget some statements that he is forced to use in C/C++. A Java programmer in C/C++ on the other hand has to use statements that he never heard of – a safe away in some disastrous results.

- The C++ compiler is nit-picking to some annoying extend. It prevents the programmer from sloppiness.

4.3   The Programming Process

How to proceed in programming an application is told to you in the programming course. But the struggle with vocabulary, concepts, and atomization of steps will sometimes hide some basic hand grips. That's why I included this short section.

4.3.1   Structured Programs

One aspect of quality management in program development is the revision of generated code by another programmer. As a beginner, you will undergo this procedure in the programming course: an experienced programmer will look over the results of some hours work of yourself and crucify it just after a few seconds being definitely not enough time to read the whole text. What an arrogant guy!

The secret of this method is that he hardly looks at the statements at the first glance but at the structure first. An example again clarifies that. Your code might look like this:

```
int main(){
int i;
int a[10];
for(i=0;i<10;i++){
a[i]=i*i; }
for(i=0;i<10;i++){
cout << a[i] << endl; }
return 0; }
```

If the task was to print out the squares of all number between 1 and 9, the program is totally correct but crucified nevertheless because it should look like this:

```
int main(){
```

```
int i;
int a[10];
for(i=0;i<10;i++){
    a[i]=i*i;
}
for(i=0;i<10;i++){
    cout << a[i] << endl;
}
return 0;
}
```

Every time a sub block is defined, the text is indented and moved out again when the block ends. When having to solve a certain problem, an experienced programmer at first generates an imagination of the principle block structure of the solution, the details coming later. This is not an extraordinary trait of a programmer: if you make a speech, you also outline at first what you want to tell your listeners before choosing the appropriate words. Some kind of structure is immanent in all languages and communication, even if we are not always aware of this.

The block structure should be visible in the program code. The experienced programmer not only has an imagination of the structure of his solution, he is also capable to evaluate the structure of other programmers whether it might fit to the problem or not. If he even doesn't find a structure in a code why bother about the rest? Here you have an answer for the crucifixion of your code.

Fortunately you will not have to reedit your code if the missing structure is criticized. Nearly every development system has an inbuilt source formatter, and you only have to search the menu where to activate it. Auto indenting is also a feature of many systems, and after a short while you will recognize the benefit of structuring yourself.

Further comments will come on the global design:

- Are 200 command lines in series really necessary? Or is the definition of some functions preferable?

  If an application or algorithm contains single algorithms or sub-algorithms, a splitting in functions (or classes) is appropriate.

- Are the application functions distributed to code functions in a useful way? Or are functions that should not be separated distributed to different functions?

  A beginner's violation of this principle is often, for example, the production of the output "Please enter some value:" in one function and reading the input in another.

- In case of object oriented programming: is the code in the proper place to make it reusable ?

  In a matrix multiplication a certain function may have been forgotten. If you now add the missing code to your main program you can neither use class internals for optimization of the algorithm nor reuse the missing code in another program.

4.3.2   Projects, Compilation, and Errors

It is possible to develop large applications only using a text editor and doing the rest in a terminal window with the help of some large manually maintained configuration files. But it is easier to use integrated development environments (IDE). Here, a graphical user interface (GUI) guides the programmer intuitively through all aspects of development.

To work with an IDE,

1. open a project,

2. create the code files.

A very often produced error of beginners is to forget 1. and begin with 2. resulting in the frustrating effect that nothing happens when he tries to start the program. Without a surrounding project nearly no IDE would work properly. The project administers the resources need by your application and tells you if something is missing. The IDE also often is able to tell you if you made grammatical errors in your code or if you are using any symbols never defined in the code. I strongly advice you to evaluate one or more IDEs to find the best one for yourself, although this is time consuming and sometimes confusing at the first glance.

In some languages like PHP the program is ready with editing the code. Others like C/C++ have to be translated to executables. In C/C++ this takes two steps:

1. A large application is often organized into many small code parts (modules), these being distributed over many files to optimize administration and re-usage. In the first step the compiler translates every code file into a binary file which is not able to run as an executable and contains symbolic links for the second process.

    In addition you may make use of libraries written by other people and provided as binary code. In order to instruct the compiler to use these functions in the right way an interface description in text form has to be included in the compiler process. In C these interface descriptions are called "header files" (in effect, the interfaces of functions in a module have also to be declared in a header file and included in all other moduls using the function).

2. When all binary files have been built faultlessly a second program, the linker, will try to tie them and some specified libraries together to the executable file.

During the process errors may occur, and here also some remarks are necessary. There are three different categories of errors:

➤   **Compiler.** If you made some errors during coding the compiler tells you in detail which lines of your code are wrong. These errors are, therefore, easy to find. There are two kinds of errors found by the compiler:

  ■   Syntax errors. You have used wrong words or forgotten a colon or something else.

  ■   Type errors. You have used incompatible data types in a command line.

  Often, the compiler finds a lot of errors. My strong advice is to care only about the first error and ignore the other ones before recompiling. In most cases these are following errors of the first one, and caring about them is often very confusing. Correct the first incident and then let the compiler again have a look at it. He will tell you where to look next.

As an example you may think of cooking something and forgetting to switch of the heater off. The first error is: food unedible, the second: pot cannot be used any longer. If you repeat the experiment now switching the heater off correctly, both errors disappear.

➤ **Linker.** If the linker cannot dissolve the internal links or does not find required functions in the libraries, a linker error is produced telling the programmer what is missing. Linker errors are much more uncomfortable than compiler errors because the linker cannot tell you where to find the reason for the error in the code. Sometimes a lot of time has to be investigated to locate the position and eliminate it.

➤ **Runtime.** The third error category is "runtime error" which may be impressive through a complete shot down of the application and some advertising windows like "this unexpected error is presented to you by Budweiser".

Even more uncomfortable are errors having no such effects but producing wrong results. Again the construction of some programming languages make it difficult for the programmer to produce errors of the first kind; errors of the second kind often imply that the programmer doesn't really understand the algorithms and perhaps should look for another job.

Nevertheless some unexpected results may appear during testing even to experienced programmers. As can easily be understood these errors should be discovered during testing: if you discover them during a test you need some time to debug your code, if your customer discovers them in his business application you need a lawyer to calm him down. So what is testing ?

✗ First you can look for the right result with some ordinary data. This is the easy task.

✗   Second you, or better another person not involved in the pro-
    gramming process, have to look out for critical data. A pro-
    gram may work with easy data but fail with critical data. You
    may cut this down to the point: first look if the program does
    its job if the user cooperates, second try all you can do to
    shut down your application.

We come back to this section later on. Now the tests show some bugs
in your code. How to find them? Two methods are widely in use and
should be used complementing each other:

- In debug mode the execution of a program can be examined
  command by command. The programmer can set break
  points where to stop the execution conditionally and inspect
  the values of the variables. This testing method may however
  take a long time in big applications.

- The programmer may insert print commands into his code to
  print out the values of certain variables. This is similar to de-
  bugging but sometimes less exhausting because needless output can be discarded easily, and called trace mode.

To debug a program a special compilation scheme must be executed
to preserve the information necessary for the debugger. This results
often in a slow execution of the application. Therefor the compiler
also provides a "release mode" besides the "debug mode". When all
tests are done the deliverable executable should be compiled in release mode; it is not seldom that this version out ranges the debug
version at a factor of 100 in execution time.

Let's stop here. There is lot more to be said on programming, for instance meta programming, that is performing algorithms on data
types instead of data during compilation. But we leave that to the
programming lessons.

4.4   Program Organization in the Memory

4.4.1   Calling a Function

To understand some principles of programming it may be helpful to know how a program is organized in the memory of a computer. Let us explain that with the help of a small code example.

```
A do_something(B b){
    int j;
    char* buffer = (char*) malloc(sizeof(A));
    A a;

    for(i=0;i<b.length();i++)
        buffer[i]=b[i];
    .. ..
    a=buffer[5];
    free(buffer);
    return a;
}


.. ..
A t;
B s;
cin >> s;
t = do_something(s);
.. ..
```

In this example a function "do_something" is defined and implemented that can be called from anywhere in the program, the function itself included. The first line – the function header or function interface – defines

a)   the name of the function to be used for calling,

b)   a call parameter of type B as input value, and

c)   a return value of type A.

Internally the function uses three temporary variables "j", "a", and "buffer", which are only defined in the actual function call. To be more precise: if the function calls itself – a process named recursion – the values of the variables in the calling instance and the called one have nothing to do with each other whatsoever.

The command lines between the last variable declaration and the return statement produce a certain value in variable "a" which shall be returned to the calling procedure. Special operations we must deal with are the calls to functions "malloc" and "free".

Let us first focus on the code storage in memory. As we know from the CPU architecture, the program counter register holds the address of the next command. When a command is executed, the next command is loaded form the memory into the operation register, optional addresses or constants are loaded too, and the program counter advances to the next command address. All commands following each other are stored successively in memory beginning at start address 0x00000000 (in effect the address differs from that value, but we ignore that here).

The function codes are also command chains placed somewhere in the memory behind the code of the main function. The address is however known to the compiler/linker so that the calls can be made to the appropriate addresses.

To install not interfering local variables the memory usage starts at the other end at address 0xFFFFFFFF and runs top down. The storage area here is called "stack", and the last address = top of stack address at entering a function is stored in a special CPU register, the stack pointer register. All local variables of a function are stored on the stack relative to this starting address (which gives reason to some other addressing mechanisms not yet discussed). Here what really is happening during a function call:

1. The input parameter values are copied to the next (lower) stack address not used by the actual function.

   This has to be done because the values are located somewhere in memory at addresses only known to the calling function but not to the called function. But the called function gets the start address of the stack at its entering point and, therefore, can now locate the values because they are located at a fixed and known offset to the stack address.

2. All registers of the CPU are pushed to the stack, the stack register is loaded with the start address as above described,

and the program counter is loaded with the first command of the function code.

This mechanism allows to continue the execution of the calling function exactly at the position and in the state that was valid when the call command was executed.

3. The function now initializes the local variables at the next stack positions using fixed offsets from the stack register address, then executes the function code, containing perhaps further function codes which are managed in the same manor.

4. Arriving at the return code, the function copies the address of the return value to the position where the calling function copied the input parameters to.

    The original return value is located somewhere on the stack, and only the called function know of the position. The input parameter position on the other hand is also known to the calling function. Placing the address (or value) here allows reading the value by the calling function.

5. All registers are read back from the stack restoring the state of the calling function before entering the called function. The calling function now can operate on the return value.

All the stack operations are managed automatically through the compiler and the runtime system. The programmer isn't forced to take any actions to get rid of variables or objects.

Between the program memory starting at 0x00000000 bottom up, and the stack memory starting at 0xFFFFFFFF top down there remains a gap not used either by program code nor stack. This memory range is call "heap" and is at the free disposition of the programmer during runtime.

"Free disposition" in reality means that the programmer can ask for memory space for certain purposes; he is not allowed to use the space without asking the system. In the code above he asks for memory by calling the method "malloc". On success the function returns an address in the heap area followed by the number of bytes specified in the function call which are reserved exclusively for the caller.

As regulation must be, the reserved memory has in the end to be given back to the system. This is done by calling the function "free". The memory now can be reserved for another process calling "malloc". The following table shows the complete overview of the memory usage by a program:

Adress 0xFFFFFFFF, Start of Stack	
Stack works up to address 0x00000000 during usage	
.. ..	
Position of variable "s" in the main program (function) section	
.. ..	
Last address used by the main program section = new value of the stack register after saving	
Complete register set of the CPU	
Copy of variable "s" from the original position on function call	Copy of variable "a" on return statement
Variable "j"	
Variable "buffer"	
Variable "a" = TOP OF STACK	
.. .. Heap area, position of the borrowed memory => "..here.."	
End of function code "do_something"	
..	
Start of function code "do_something"	
.. other functions ..	

| END OF PROGRAM |
| .. code of main section .. |
| Adress 0x00000000: Start of main section |

Let's add some remarks on errors. Perhaps the reader already heard of one or another:

✗   If you forget to free a heap variable, you produce a so called **memory leak**. If you remember the function call mechanism, the address (the address, not the value!) of a heap variable is stored in a local function variable. On leaving the function the local variable address is no longer available, and so is the address of the heap variable. The space is occupied, but nobody has a chance to free it.

   If this happens several times and the application runs for a long time like servers, the heap is completely filled with occupied but unused space, then the disk is filled by a growing swap file, and then the systems stops and can sometimes only be recovered by "format c:".

✗   If you try to write outside the reserved space the system may

   •   fire you immediately (segmentation fault, we noticed that already), or

   •   fire you on deleting the heap variable (corrupted memory exception).

✗   If you try to write outside the space of a variable with other variables surrounding it you will invoke a **buffer overlow** meaning you have changed the value stored on a variable you didn't want to touch. Most times the system will not recognize that, but hackers do and will find some way to hijack your system.

   Such errors appear if you reserve an array with, say, 10 elements and try to write data to index 15.

These mechanisms apply to nearly all programming languages some of which hiding more details from the programmer (Java, for instance, does not allow to make very dangerous errors and throws an exception, but you must pay for this "security" with execution time. C on the other hand is far faster then Java but you have to pay with a greater amount of caution during the coding process). The drawn picture is of course too simple if we refer to object oriented techniques, but is sufficient for a principle understanding of memory management.

> **Exercise.** This exercise requires programming knowledge in C++. Just implement a class with a constructor, a copy constructor, and a destructor, each with a "cout" line inside to observe when a function is called. Implement a function taking a class object as parameter and returning a class object. Interpret the "cout" messages in terms of the above description.

4.4.2 Parameter delivery Methods

In the last chapter we delivered the value of a variable by copying it to a stack position known to both functions. This sometimes has some drawbacks:

- The called function cannot alter the value in the scope of the calling function because it is a copy, not the original.

- If the value is large, for example, the complete content of a book, the copy operation takes a lot of time and consumes a lot of memory.

To deal with this drawbacks the language developers have introduced some tricks in the calling mechanism:

- **Call by value.** The explicit value of a variable is copied to the stack as we have described in our example.

  This method is only necessary when the value must be altered in the called function but has to remain constant in the calling function. It should be restricted to these cases.

- **Call by reference.** The address of the original variable is copied to the stack. An address is only 32 or 64 bit long and, therefore, much shorter as most objects. The speed of operation increases accordingly.

The method can be subdivided into to types:

○ **Constant reference.** The value is not changed inside the called function. Some compilers allow the declaration of constant references and refuse compilation when the programmer tries to alter the value of a constant reference parameter.

○ **Reference.** A reference parameter not declared constant can be altered inside the called function, and contains, therefore, another value when the control returns to the calling function. Besides the return value this is another way to export calculation results from a function.

Something similar can also be used by return statements. It is clear from the above discussion that a local variable of a function cannot be returned by a reference because in the next function call the memory will be used by another function and the values are lost. But we have learned that it is possible to lean memory from the system getting only the address in the heap range. This address can of course be delivered to the calling function. On doing so the responsibility for giving back the memory to the system is transferred to the calling function which must call the system function "free" when the variable is no longer needed.

Again not all languages support all mechanisms, and they use different automation strategies hiding parts of actions from the programmer.

Exercise. Expand the last exercise to reference or constant reference in the parameter call and return of a pointer.

4.5   Testing, and Optimization

First versions of a program are neither very elegant nor error tolerant. The next step is, therefore, testing. What is testing? When I criticize a beginner's program, I often here the argument *"what do you want from me? The program is running."* At one occasion the root of a number had to be calculated, and on entering the number 9 I got the result 6.13. The student informed me that this was my fault(!). If I would have taken the input 25 , the program would have returned the correct result 5 . The program was running, what else?

Testing means something other than providing the program with some complaisance input. In a real test the tester should think about how to fool the program (and in industrial tests the tester is not the programmer, often even not a programmer himself). What are inputs that might not have been considered by the programmer, who always uses an optimal input during construction?

Here are the rules: if you are the tester and a program is send to the desert by your input choice, give it just back to the programmer along with the input which caused the error. Don't try to analise the code! You are the tester, not the quality manager looking for program structure, code elegance, and coherent object structure. That's the job of someone other. Give it just back and start again with <u>all test cases</u> in the next trial, even those the program has passed before, because it might be that the repair operation results in opening a trap again that was closed in a run before.

Exercise. Some traps in the first algorithm written in daily language are already mentioned in the description, but there are a lot more. Try to find and eliminate them. Good luck (and good night until tomorrow)!

If you are sure to the out most extent that your program really does under all circumstances what is should do, you may start to optimize it. It is advisable to eliminate flaws first, because you then have a reference program you can test your optimization against. It is also recommended to list all test cases and apply them all to optimized versions of the program.

Optimizations can be tried out in several directions:

- In the daily language example we operate with "goto" instead of loops using "while" or "for". Higher computer languages contain a lot of phrases to make the work flow more clear and the programming less error vulnerable.

- We also used "goto" instead of "call ... return". Defining functions make their code reusable.

- You can try to regroup data structures and code, the working field of object oriented programming.

- You can think about better resource usage, for instance

  ○ to develop an algorithm that does the same job in a fraction of the time, or

  ○ an algorithm that uses only a fraction of the memory of the original algorithm.

The results of optimization processes can be very impressive. Encryption algorithms for instance need to be highly optimized because they have to handle with large amounts of data in real time. The NIST has chosen the standard algorithms to be used in web applications in an open competition, the last being a competition to define a new standard for hash algorithms. About 100 algorithms were submitted and intensively tested. They can easily be found through a search on the web, and the interesting part is the code itself. Each algorithm comes along with a reference implementation reflecting directly the theory used. But each algorithm also provides one or several optimized versions, often specialized optimizations for a specific hardware. If you put the codes side by side, it is in a lot of cases hard to see that they should really do the same thing. But these are some extreme examples admittedly.

Exercise. If you have got some experience with a programming language in the meantime, try to implement a sophisticated optimized version of our daily language example.

4.6   Complexity of Computing

4.6.1   Conceptual Explanation

How long does it take the computer to solve the problem? The question is of high importance because the programmer most often tests his work using a love letter of some pages and the customer tries the same operation on the complete text of the Bible. The customer perhaps may feel that it is really time for a job to terminate that runs in real time under laboratory conditions.

Theoretical Informatics has defined the term "complexity" for this symptom (in fact, complexity is a lot more than we discuss here). The simplest explanation may be:

> If n is a measure for the amount of input, how do computing time and memory usage vary with n ?

The answer is often given in terms of "order of complexity", in mathematics, for example, by

$$O(n^2)$$

The meaning is: if you double the amount of input, the computing time (or memory usage) is forth the original time (quadratic growing). Example: if n is the number of equations in a system of linear equations, the memory to store all coefficients is proportional to n^2 .

The order is defined as "asymptotic order". For instance you may derive for a certain problem that the calculation time grows according to

$$t = 37*n^3 + 12*n^2 + 185$$

If n gets big enough, all terms but the third power have almost no influence on the further growth of the computing time. And because the factor 37 is also uninteresting (a colleague may develop an algorithm with factor 29 at this position), the order is simply

$$O(n^3)$$

If you have determined the order of an algorithm, a breakdown due to few testing data during development followed by large application data sets from the customer shouldn't occur, because if you know of a high order you will surely ask the customer what he wants to do and advice him to choose the appropriate application.

The abstract concept of order seems to be very easy to apply to practice, but this isn't true at any rate because of the asymptotic evaluation. If you have developed two algorithms with different order, it is not always wise to take that one with lesser order. Perhaps the second algorithm consumes time in detail according to

$$t = 2 * n^4 + 2$$

and it can clearly be seen that this algorithm behaves far better than the first one if only n rests small enough.

As a conclusion we have to note: for each algorithm we have to determine its order of complexity, but for the decision which one to deliver to the customer, we also have to analyze his problem and probable have to make some laboratory measurements.

4.6.2   Loops, and Complexity

We have already introduced/used loops in an intuitive way, and perhaps they have already been explained in the programming course, therefore, the concept should be known to you. It is very simple to evaluate the order of an algorithm counting loops. The time consumption of the loop

```
for(i=0;i<n;i++)  …
```

grows linearly with n , therefore, the order of the algorithm is $O(n)$. The same is true for

```
for(i=0;i<n;i++) { .. }
for(k=0;k<n;k++) { .. }
```

because both loops don't interact; the order is always $O(n)$.

In the last paragraph of the previous chapter we have noted that the exact behavior should be known in some cases, therefore, you may be tempted to analyze the inner life of the loops to determine the co-efficients by theory. Often this is wasted time: if the compiler opti-mizes the machine code, the results depend on the strategies imple-mented during compiler development, and if some libraries are used to do some work, the same applies to them.

Although is may be not easy – modern computer hardware is very fast, and time measurement has to be in the order of seconds to get meaningful results – the suitable method to acquire the exact time dependence is measurement. At least some basic measurement may be necessary anyway to estimate the time consumption of the cus-tomer's jobs.

> **Exercise.** If you are already familiar with a programming lan-guage, execute some experiments to verify the orders of different loop designs.

Back to basic calculation of the order. If the loops interact, the above story changes:

```
for(i=0;i<n;i++) {
    for(k=0;k<n;k++) { .. }
}
```

In this example the inner loop grows linearly for each cycle of the outer loop which also grows linearly. Putting both things together we arrive in fact at the order $O(n^2)$. The general rule is, therefore,e very simple:

> The nesting depth of loops is the power of the order.

But be careful! This holds only when all loops alter with n. Two ex-amples:

Example 1

```
for(i=0;i<n;i++) {
    for(k=0;k<5;k++) { .. }
}
```

Example 2

```
for(i=0;i<n;i++) {
    for(k=0;k<i;k++) { .. }
```

}

The nesting depth is two for both examples. But in example 1, the inner loop doesn't vary with n , therefore, the total order is $O(n)$. In the second example the inner loop varies with n , and if you use some maths, you will find that the number of loop cycles can be calculated by

$$1+2+3+...+n=\frac{n*(n-1)}{2}$$

So in fact, the order of example 2 is $O(n^2)$. The time doesn't grow as fast as in the first nested loop example, but the construction if nevertheless of the same order.

Exercise. One algorithm often treated already in high school is the Gauss' Algorithm to solve linear equations. Finger out the order of the algorithm.

Remark: you don't need to be able to implement the algorithm in a computer language. Math will do. A little help: the first part – diagonalization of the matrix – is one order higher than the backward elimination.

4.6.3   An Example from Cryptography

If n is the interesting quantity itself and all is done directly in the loops, the determination of the order isn't a great thing. But often functions are called inside the loops whose time consumption is a function of n too, and n may itself not be the interesting quantity itself, but a function of n. This makes the determination of the order difficult, and even for a trained computer scientist it may be very problematic to understand why a mathematician arrives at terms like

$$O(\exp(n*\log n*\log\log n))$$

in the evaluation of an algorithm. Here comes a short but simple example for such calculations.

In cryptography the "amount of input" is often measured in the number of bits used for encryption. To break the widely used RSA cryptographic method which is often used in SSL/TLS, we have to find out the prime factors of a big number of some 1,024 – 2,048 bits in size (meaning: the number is in the magnitude of $2^{1,024}$ that is a number having about 300 decimal digits; an example was already presented in the number chapter).

The simplest method for factorization is probe division: you try all small prime numbers until you find a factor. In the worst case – the number only has two factors, which are of similar magnitude – all numbers in the interval

$$3 \leq F \leq \sqrt{N}$$

have to be tested with $N \sim 2^n$.

Exercise. The first shot of the number interval often ends at $N/2$, but in fact the root which has only have of the digits of N is sufficient. Explain this.

For specialists: what about Ns with more than two factors?

The primary order is, therefore, (using some mathematic equalities to get a term containing the input measure "bits used")

$$O(\sqrt{N}) = O(\exp(1/2 * \log(N))) = O(e^n)$$

If we take into account that multiplication/division requires two nested loops the upper limit being the number of digits, the complete complexity grows to

$$O(\exp(n * \log(n)))$$

That is why cryptography is safe. The time for breaking RSA using this algorithm grows exponentially in then number of bits used, and you can easily run away ("better" algorithms are not far better up to now).

Math is a devil's factory, as the following short story tells: some years ago, 1,024 bit were used for RSA numbers, and the best cracking method could factorize numbers in the order of 512 bit. Then a researcher announced that he had developed an algorithm twice as fast as the best before. Great panic in the web! *"Twice as fast! Are 2,048 bits as key length sufficient? Or is it better to change to 4,096?"*

Great Panic for nothing. We are talking about the amount of bits used for a number. An algorithm being twice as fast as before can break 513 bit numbers in the same time, the old one did with 512 bit numbers. So be aware of math!

Exercise. It's time to use some other sources of information, too. RSA uses exponentiation. It is easy to verify that

$$8187279719792739847917293 7^{9038409820983094809238 40982}$$

isn't solvable by using a loop multiplying a number 9038409820983094809238 40982-times with itself. An exponentiation algorithms only uses about 90 loop cycles to finish the job. Try to find this algorithm in the web!

---

5   Some Hardware Devices

We have discussed logic circuits, bus systems, memory devices, and clocks so far. But modern computers are not thinkable without further devices for persistent mass data storage, graphical displays, communication facilities, and other devices. We take a short look at the technologies of such devices, but only to achieve a basic understanding.

5.1   The Processing Unit and Mainboard

Modern miniaturization techniques allow for denser placement of devices on the boards which results in an increase of speed (we already mentioned Moore's Law). But since 2009 a barrier seems to have been reached: the frequency of operation could only be increased in very small portions (see "Bus Systems" later on), and an increase the of circuits building up a processing unit only results in increased heat loss but hardly in increased computing power. So how Moore's Law can by valid nevertheless?

A Central Processing Unit or CPU today is in most cases not a single CPU but consists of 2-16 independent CPU Kernels. The CPU designers already noticed in 2,004 or so that further architectural growth of a single CPU wouldn't be the solution for a further increase of computing power according to Moore's Law. Several smaller individual CPUs occupying the same area have a bigger potential.

When one CPU in such multi-kernel processors is occupied by some hard calculations taking several clock cycles on the bus, other CPUs can meanwhile read or write their data. But that's not the only trick. Each kernel, or at least a small group of kernels, owns its own cache. A cache is a small amount of a very fast memory device. In modern Intel P7 CPUs there are three cache levels:

- L1 cache: each kernel 32 + 32 KiB (data + instructions)

- L2 cache: each kernel 256KiB driven by CPU clock

- L3 cache: 4,096 KiB driven by bus clock

A CPU is about a 1,000 times faster than the ability of the RAM to deliver data to the CPU. Each cache level is about 10 times faster than the lower level, and when the CPU is working on one part of it's L1 cache, the other parts can be transfered from and to the L2 cache, and so on. Surely a certain strategy of consuming and producing data must be present to achieve best operations times.

To sum up: the speed of execution of a single serial program increases only in small portions, but the computers have gained the ability to operate on several serial programs at the same time, so Moore's Law is fulfilled.

But the software engineer can also take an active role in the game. Why should he restrict himself on serial program architectures when more than one kernel is available? Thus, hardware technology has also a deep impact on software technology because software has to be constructed in a way to support parallel programming on several levels, and the speed a single application is executed with may also follow Moore's Law to some extend. Sure there are some difficulties left:

- Some algorithms do not allow for parallelism, and such applications cannot be made much faster.

- As far as now most languages are a little bit inadequate for the task because parallelism is not part of the grammar itself. May be that changes in the future.

But the technique doesn't stop here: connection networks can be used to connect several mainboards to even lager systems. We come back to this in another chapter, and the principles are discussed in detail in a lesson about "Parallel Programming".

5.2   Persistent Disk Storage

To store a program and data in the memory, at least a small special program is needed to do that, the basic input output system BIOS. It can for instance be used to read data from a keyboard and store them in specified memory addresses, or send the computation results to a printer. The BIOS is, therefore, a small program itself which has to be developed (only) once and has to be hard wired to be present whenever the computer is started. For these purposes special "read only" memory devices (ROM) were developed, which occur in one of three types:

a) The program is part of the circuit design.

b) The device is completely filled with 1 bits, and the program is written to the device once by destroying electrical micro wires at the 0 bit positions by a special programming voltage.

c) The device contains special transistor types which can be "programmed" to special behavior by a programming voltage, which can be erased with UV light. The devices allow multiple programming cycles (EPROM, Figure 5.1).

Figure 5.1: EPROM

Modern micro computer exercise boards only have few functions more than reading something from a keyboard, and application programs are burned in an EPROM. Such a strategy is, however, only suitable for small systems with only one firm task.

Figure 5.2: 500 GB hard disk

In most computers, the BIOS' job is to load the operating and other software from persistent hard disk drives. A hard disk is build of one or more magnetic disks rotating at high speed and two read/write heads for each disk which can be moved over the surface by a high precision step motor (Figure 5.2, Figure 5.3). The disk is magnetized according to the bit patterns to be stored. The surface has to be extremely smooth because the head is only prevented from crushing the magnetic layer by the air cushion produced by the rotating speed.

The technology comes from audio data storage on magnetic tapes, and the first steps were also taken with tapes. Audio recordings must allow for a high frequency range which also allows for dense storing of digital data. Tapes have the disadvantage to be only readable sequentially. If data have to be fetched from somewhere else on the tape in an operation comparable to a function call in a program, the tape has to be winded and the position to be searched, which take a long processing time.

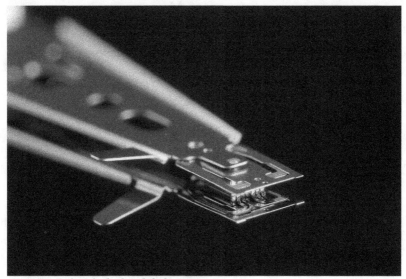

Figure 5.3: head of a hard disk

In principle, the same operation has to be made on a disk, but the re-
striction of "tape length" to one disc rotation cycle and the position-
ing of the R/W head on different "tapes" by a step motor makes the
search operation much faster. The technique evolved from the first
floppy disks of some 100 kBytes (10^5) to modern hard disks containing several tera bytes (10^{12}).

To localize data on the disks the space addressing is organized in sectors, tracks, and heads. The head, and track number organization is
trivially given by hardware, the sector organization is a little bit more
complicated.

In Figure 5.4, A is a track, B is a physical sector, C the storage sector
as a combination of both, and D a storage block spanning over 3 sectors. To identify a sector the sector borders contain a special magnetic coding scheme which cannot in stored data and can, therefore,
be reliably detected. One of these borders contains a special start
coding, and therefore, the controller is able to count reliably the sectors of the track. The combination

```
Head / Track / Sector in Track / Byte in Sector
```

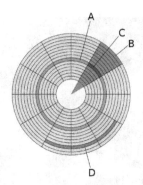

Figure 5.4: organization of disks

now precisely indicate every byte even on tera byte disks. Such amounts of data need further organization which is done by the operating system OS. We will discuss their function in a later chapter.

Exercise. If a disk has 2 heads, 200 tracks, and 32 sectors of 512 bytes in each track, how many bytes can be stored? Where can you find byte no. 2,377,128,911?

Some 20 years ago, all this was managed by the CPU itself, but modern technology knows division of labor. Specialized micro computer controllers manage the disk system hiding completely the exact details of head/track/sector-structure from the operating system which can use more simple addressing schemes instead of taking into account special disk manufacturer's specifications.

Due to the hardware organization scheme a head reads a complete track each time a specific byte is asked for by the application. Data are organized in logical blocks varying with device which applies for the operating system, too: the disk controller always exchanges a complete block with the operating system, even if only a specific byte is needed by the application (a block may be the number of bytes in a physical sector, but that is not an imperative rule). This putative disadvantage can be turned in an advantage: all entities can store several blocks in RAM which is far more faster than a physical disk operation, and if another byte is requested no further read operation is necessary. Write operations can also be delayed in the same manor to increase the total throughput. Modern disk controllers additionally measure statistics of the blocks requested to predict which bytes would probably be asked for in then next operation. The belonging tracks are read in in advance.

The life time of disks as mixed mechanical devices is limited, and the controller also measures statistics of errors:

- A signal has to observe specific levels to be clearly defined. If it is ambiguous, the sector is reread and the number of reread-operations is counted.

- The data bytes are secured by check sums which spread out from parity checks of a few bits over CRC checksum of a sector up to md5 hash values of bigger structures. Some of these check sums are constructed in a way to allow the repair of some error types.

- If errors in a sector sum up to a certain value, the sector is marked "unusable" and a reserve sector is used instead.

Modern disks reserve a specific number of sectors as reserve sectors, and switching from a broken sector to a reserve sector is done transparently for the OS which has not to take care of such internals. If all reserved sectors are used, the disk is at the end of its life time because the next failure cannot be managed. Operating systems do in most cases not warn the user of this automatically! You need to start special applications to read out the SMART values of the disk, and it is recommended to do so regularly to prevent from bad news about your data.

Additional techniques are known as RAID systems: several disks are bundled by a RAID controller. The purpose can be

- **Safety of the data.** the data are stored on more than one disk. If one disk turns to machined mode and the head destroys the magnetic surface, the data stored on the backup disk are available.

- **Speed.** Data are spread over several disks. If one disk is occupied by a read/write operation, the requested data are probably on another disk which can handle the request.

- **Mixed** versions of speed and safety.

RAID controlling is also done transparently. The OS must not take care of this but just handle disk operations in the same manor as without RAID technology.

Similar to magnetic disk storage is optical storage on CDs oder DVDs. These devices however act on low speed compared to hard disks, offer less amount of memory and support only one direction at a time (in most cases only read operations). The media themselves are very robust and can be exchanged between different R/W devices.

5.3   Bus Systems

We have spoken simply about a data bus so far as a bundle of wires connecting the CPU with the memory devices. Concerning small micro computers, this image is mostly sufficient, but on modern computers we have to take into account special physical laws.

Principally there are the following possibilities:

- **parallel transport**: each bit is transported over its own wire, and all bits are send at the same time and arrive at the same time at the destination , or

- **serial transport**: the bits are serialized with a clock, send over one single wire, and have to be reassembled at the target position.

At the first glance, parallel transport should be faster than serial transport, although the expenditure is a manifold of the serial transport version. But the situation becomes more complex if we take into account the real transport speed and the physical dimensions of the system.

Modern computers are operating in the GHz scale, and the following diagram shows the dependency of frequency and wavelength (and other tasks to be taken into consideration).

		VHF	UHF	L	S	C	X	Ku	K	Ka	Millimeter			sichtbares		
	D (alt)	VHF	UHF	L	S	C	X	Ku	K	Ka	Millimeter			sichtbares Licht		
	USA (alt)	I G P	L	S	C X	K	Q V	W				IR			UV
Frequenz in GHz		0,2 0,25 0,5	1,0	2 3 4	6 810	20	40 60 100								
	Europa (neu)	A B	C	D	E F G H I	J	K	L	M			IR			UV
Wellenlänge in cm	300 150	60	30	15 7,5 5	3	1,5	0,75 0,5 0,3				0,00005				

Figure 5.5: frequency ranges

The values apply to vacuum conditions, but the maximum speed of wire signals is significantly lower than vacuum light speed, the wave-length, therefore, being less.

If you have a look at data sheets of electronic devices, we often see di-agrams like this one:

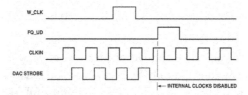

Signals on the bus are shown to be rectangular, and the presence of a signal at the source and the destination is assumed to be simultane-ous. But this is an idealization. In the frequency diagram we can ob-serve that the CPU clock speed is in the order of radio or television signals. High frequency signals being put on a wire result in antenna effects: the wire looses electrical power through radiation, and a ra-dio signal can be recognized in the surrounding. As the first conse-quence, the devices must be encapsulated to prevent the environ-ment from electrical pollution, and all devices have to pass EMV tests before being distributed.

The antenna effects have a second outcome: the neighboring wire also behaves like an antenna and a portion of the signal can be ob-served on the neighbor. The effect increases with frequency, and to prevent from ghost signals of the neighbor the wires in modern bus systems are separated by mass wires which absorb the ghost effects. As a consequence, the expenditure increases again: instead of 32 wires, 64 are needed for the mass separation.

But this is not the end of the line: if the frequency grows further, the signal of the source might have been already cut off before the front of the wave is reaching the destination, and the signal form is not longer rectangular but some kind of sine wave with low defined edges. If some of the parallel wires are slightly longer than others due to ranging conditions on the ground plate, a signal might not be clearly defined when the clock signal opens the window for executing the read/write operation, and an error is encountered.

From these observations we can derive the conclusion that parallel data buses are not only limited by the expenditure for the wiring, but their usable speed is also limited by a relationship between frequency and system dimensions. Let's put it together:

Conclusion for the overall speed

The CPU dimension is small and, therefore, in most cases uncritical, and the frequency of the inner CPU clock can be rather high.

On the other hand, the higher the frequency the more the energy dissipation due to radiation and other physical effects. The increase in CPU frequency will eventually lead to heat problems instead of speed enlargement, and here will be a border line of useful frequency too.

Another limiting aspect of CPU speed is the speed of the outer bus system: it is of no value to increase the speed of the CPU to an amount that it has to spend more than 50% of time by waiting on the lower devices.

Conclusion for system architecture

In mid range a parallel bus has advantages in overall speed over serial devices out ranging the expenditure. Motherboards, therefore, are wired with parallel buses, but the maximum bus frequency is significantly below the possible CPU frequency.

Some memory, the so called cache, is, therefore, placed on the CPU itself, and a lot of software strategies occupy with the questions which memory information is used more often than others and should be placed in the cache instead of the ordinary ram.

Long range connection, including the hard disk, is better suited by serial connections. The frequency usable in modern techniques out ranges the possible speed of parallel buses of that length.

The hard disks are usually connected with the special high speed SATA bus, whereas other devices like mouse, keyboard, printer, or others that do not need high speed connections and are separated several feet from the main computer, make use of the slower USB bus which allows the connection of several devices simultaneously and is controlled by special micro controllers.

Exercise. Words, words, words! A graphic often tells more than a thousand words, and presentation techniques are included in technical studies too today. Try to draw some presentation sheets showing the contexts and the limits.

5.4   Graphic Controller and Display

Graphic cards come with their own processors known as GPUs (Graphical Processing Unit). GPUs are based on another computing concept: whereas CPUs are designed for serial execution of program code, GPUs are massive parallel computers consisting of several thousand stream processors managed by a supervisor engine (Figure 5.6).

The theory of computer graphic is rather simple: objects are stored as sets of points in a three dimensional space with additional properties like lines defined between two points, planes defined by three points, inner and outer surface of a plane with additional material properties, and some further special traits. Different light sources illuminate the virtual world, and a virtual camera is looking at the scene from some arbitrary coordinates. To produce an image on the display the processor has to calculate which parts of an object are visible, which parts are hidden by another object, has to consider shadows or mirror effects, perspectives, and so on (Figure 5.7).

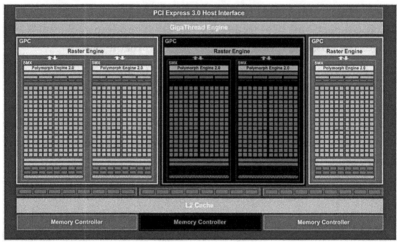

Figure 5.6: GPU design principle (NVidia)

Although this may sound complicated, especially when you think about some 100,000 points a scene consist of, the theory is mostly limited to simple linear algebra and some principles of projective geometry. In 99,9% of all calculations only floating point calculation and addition is necessary, enveloped in some large loops. The only problem is the mass of calculations to be done, but most calculations are independent from each other, and that's why they can be executed on different devices at the same time. This allows for the special hardware design of a GPU. A GPU is constructed to execute a small set of instructions at high speed and in parallel execution pipelines, but for instance doesn't know what to do with an IF..THEN..ELSE.. decision.

GPUs keep to follow Moore's Law of doubling their speed every two years up to now, in contrast to CPUs. The manufactures increase the numbers of parallel kernels every year because the calculation principles allow for that. The software engineers follow these lines: today real time 3D games are very impressive compared to the games a few years ago, but they often require the latest hardware to function properly.

In modern entertainment the impacts are even beyond pure computer graphics: it is possible to record the exact patterns of movement of a person from a special video sequence, and in some modern

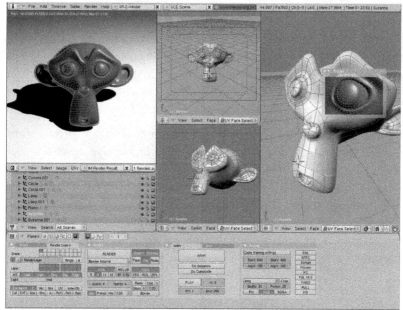

Figure 5.7: example of graphical editor

movies the actors don't act directly but are simulated by computer graphics up to a perfection that the viewer doesn't realize it. The expenditure is, however, enormous. Clusters of highly specialized computers are occupied with such calculations for months.

5.5   Supercomputers and other trends

Supercomputers take a further step in parallelism of calculations: they don't constrain on multi kernel mainboards to speed up applications, they don't stop at connecting a greater amount of such mainboars with high speed connection networks, they also combine CPUs and GPUs to heterogeneous hardware devices to achieve extreme calculation power. To bring it to a simple sheme:

- CPUs care about all kind of decisions link IF.. which influence the direction of the calculation,

- GPUs are doing the standard calculations not being influenced by intermediate results.

To get an impression of the performance achievable: a high class standard PC is operating at 45 Gflops/sec (floating point operations), supercomputers do up to 33,500 Tflops/sec, that is about 1,000,000 times the calculating power of a PC. Sure, they can do that only on application problems allowing for parallelism.

Is it a good idea to deal with such techniques in an introductory book? Yes, indeed, because the good and impressive news are that you can do all kind of exercises on parallel computing on your own pc or notebook because the necessary frameworks are part of the operating systems today. The keywords are OpenMPI, OpenMP, and OpenCL (and some further). You may occupy yourself with parallel programming of you don't have the patience to wait for a special reading.

Another future technique may be the transition from electrical to optical devices. Optical devices are not sensitive to the electrical effects we have described and can operate at far higher speed. Serial versions of optical bus systems may be more efficient than electrical parallel buses, and therefore, the data bus will no longer be the bottleneck of computation. It is also possible to think of the doubling the number of bus lines on the board because optical systems need not to be shielded.

Whether logical CPU circuits can be constructed from optical devices is another question to be solved. An intermediate way may be to implement a bulk serial optical buses to supply an increased number of kernels with data. What exactly will be the line of development lies in the dark of the future. But be assured by an old guy: it will be very interesting.

Students often ask about the possibilities of quantum computing, or some similar stuff appearing in literature. These techniques are not universal ,and likely not scalable, too, even if the scientists concerned with these techniques spread optimism (have in mind: they must do so! Nobody would give them money for their research if they come up with the news "very interesting, but probably not usable"). Up to now, only a few very special algorithms have been developed for quantum computers – in theory! No one really knows whether an operating quantum computer will really be build in the future – I doubt it for theoretical reasons concerning scalability. The most important point of view to ignore such techniques for the moment: quantum computers relay on completely other physical basics than electronic computers. You can't understand them without some deep insights in quantum mechanics.

6   Operating System

We have only talked about application programs so far. Applications should calculate special things regardless of the hardware provided and should not interfere with other applications. On the other hand, modern machines have enough calculating power to handle multiple applications at a time, therefore, they should provide mechanisms to support this. To manage these requirement an operating system (OS) is necessary.

Operating systems have a lot of things to manage, and they come along with a lot of standard applications. The OS with all its parts is stored on the hard disk as any other application program, and the parts needed for system operation have to be loaded before any application can do its work.

6.1   Loading the OS

The job of the BIOS, a small program we mentioned earlier, is to load the OS into the memory. In order to find the OS on the disk it has to know the disk organization.

The disk space is organized in large blocks called partitions. Whereas the entire disk is a physical device, a partition is a logical device. A disk can contain several partitions which

- allows for faster operations,

- allows for better organization and migration of the user data, and

- allows the installation of several different OS.

One partition is marked "startable" which means that it contains an OS. The BIOS looks up that partition in the partition table and starts the OS. If several different OSs are installed on a disk, a boot loader takes over the role and is started first. It allows to choose an OS to start.

A special disk sector in the start partition, the boot sector, tells the BIOS where to find the special loader of the OS on the disk. This relative small part has an absolute address on the disk and is loaded into the memory and started as the first application. It has the function of the special OS loader because it knows from the installation process which parts of the OS should be loaded.

The OS loader now loads and tests all parts of the OS, sometimes with the help of a RAM disk because the full operating disk drivers are not yet loaded. The loaded parts of the OS can be differentiated in the kernel and a lot of ordinarily behaving processes similar to application processes. We describe the attributes of both in the following sections. Every loaded part first executes some tests on the devices it should serve and loads additional configuration data or calculates them. The large number of devices causes a large number of processes, and some additional management work causes a rather long time until the OS is ready for the user.

6.2   The Kernel

If a function has to be called within a program, the starting address of the function code is loaded into the program counter register along with some other work. But how can a function be called in another application? The codes have been compiled individually and nobody knows of the internals of the other code. And how can a device like the hard disk signal that data are available for a certain application?

The answer is a hardware trick named interrupt. An interrupt is a signal to the CPU to stop all pending work and start a special function which handles the interrupt. The handling has to be rather short. It should consume less time than the interval between incoming interrupts. After finishing the interrupt request the interrupted command sequence is resumed at the position that it was stopped.

The CPU knows of a set of hardware initiated interrupts which are initiated by certain states of hardware devices, and a set of software interrupts which are executed by special commands in an application code, so called interrupt requests IRQ. A hardware IRQ initiates the following sequence:

a) The interrupt controller checks whether the interrupt is allowed to occur. If the IRQ is masked, the request is marked as pending and activated when the mask is erased.

   If more than one IRQ is pending when execution becomes permitted, the IRQ with the highest priority is served first and the others are queued again.

b) On executing an IRQ all others are masked out (with minor exceptions). The CPU is switched to absolute addressing mode (we will explain that later on), and at least the program counter is saved on the stack.

c) The IRQ number specifies the index in a (hardware defined) address table starting at position 0x00000000. The OS stores the addresses of the interrupt handling routines here during the boot process. This address is loaded to the program counter and the function is executed. All primary interrupt handler routines are part of the OS kernel.

d) The function has to save all other registers that are needed inside the function on the stack, too. As an option further IRQ may be allowed.

e) After finishing the IRQ processing the function reads the saved registers from the stack and executed a "return from interrupt" command which inverts action b). The interrupted code gets control again and is in the state it had when the interrupt occurred.

Software interrupts are managed in a similar way except that the return sequence differs in some events. If the software interrupt is a signal of the initiating process to ask for some services of another process, the kernel initiates the execution of the service instead of returning back to the initiating process. This happens later on when the service is ready.

To realize this the kernel manages a list of all processes loaded into memory. As we know from experience, a computer seems to be able to execute several applications simultaneously. This is achieved by the hardware clock (this is not the clock responsible for the command execution ticks!) which delivers a non maskable interrupt every 20 ms. A part of the kernel – the scheduler – switches at this intervals from process to process allowing each to run only a short time. 20 ms switch time are very short for man, and therefore, we perceive the execution simultaneous.

Back to the process list. Every process in the scheduler's list can appear in one of the following states:

- **Idle.** The process is loaded but not active. This applies to most OS processes because they are needed by application processes to execute special services on demand. They are loaded to memory to speed up operation; otherwise they would have to be loaded in a time consuming operation from the hard disk each time they are called.

- **Waiting.** These processes wait for execution during one of the coming time slots. There are multiple strategies to decide which waiting process should be activated next, for example, a down counter is started when a process enters the waiting state, and the process with the lowest counter is started next.

- **Executing.** This is the process just running when the clock signal generates an IRQ.

- **Locked.** These processes wait for some other processes to end execution. For example, an application can wait for the disk process to fetch the disk data and the disk process signals the kernel upon returning where to find the data and which process to reactivate.

```
A process list:
---------------
  PID TTY          TIME CMD
    1 ?        00:00:01 init
    2 ?        00:00:00 kthreadd
    3 ?        00:00:07 ksoftirqd/0
    5 ?        00:00:00 kworker/0:0H
```

```
 7 ?              00:00:00 kworker/u:0H
 8 ?              00:00:00 migration/0
 9 ?              00:00:00 rcu_bh
10 ?              00:00:12 rcu_sched
11 ?              00:00:00 watchdog/0
12 ?              00:00:00 watchdog/1
13 ?              00:00:06 ksoftirqd/1
14 ?              00:00:00 migration/1
16 ?              00:00:00 kworker/1:0H
17 ?              00:00:00 cpuset
```

A typical software IRQ demanding for data from the hard disk may now be handled like this:

a) The kernel knows from the IRQ number the called process and transfers the data and the process number of the requesting service to it. The state of the requesting process is saved on the stack, the process marked "lock", and the called process activated (in case of a system process with high priority; if the process is already active from another call, that new call is queued).

b) The data transfer between the disk and the service process is initiated. The complete execution may need hardware interrupts, too.

c) After having finished the disk handling the disk service signals this to the kernel by another IRQ. The kernel then transfers the data to the calling process and mark it "waiting" again so that the scheduler can activate it.

6.3   Memory Managing Unit

The last functional description contains some further secrets paraphrased with "*the kernel transfers the data from process to process*" which are to be opened now.

Starting with many processes of the operating system, nobody knows where an application is loaded into the memory. From our discussion of programming we know, however, that the addresses of functions and variables must be known to the code in order to function properly. If you think about this problem, you may have the idea that the operating system recalculates all addresses in the applications before loading the application in the memory. But besides time losses this would not be fault tolerant, therefore, the engineers have chosen an‑other strategy:

1. The kernel of the OS is the only program in the whole system using absolute adresses,

2. all other application codes use the logical address interval 0x00000000 – 0xFFFFFFFF (or whatever the total address range will be) they were coded for during compilation and linking, but are located on arbitrary free memory positions by the kernel.

How to achieve this? The trick is a memory usage table which is man‑aged by the kernel. The memory is managed in blocks or pages of, say, 1,024 bytes which means that 0.1% of the memory space is used for such a page table. The page size is a compromise between effective management (small pages result in a big table) and few wasted loca‑tions (an application may use only some bytes of a page).

If an application is to be loaded, the OS reads out the information from the program file, which memory portion is at least necessary for the program to run. For example, the program demands

```
0x000000 - 0x008FFF :  code area
0x009000 - 0xFFFFFF :  global symbols
0x8FFFFF - 0xFFFFFF :  primary stack range
```

The OS now looks at its memory usage tables whether enough space is available. If the application can be loaded, it gets a process number (PID) and the necessary pages are reserved for the process and loaded with the code. A special hardware device, the memory man‑agement unit MMU, holds the table with all information necessary:

```
PID      Real Block          Virtual Address
------------------------------------------------
1017     0x00F               0x000000 - 0x000FFF
1017     0X012               0x001000 - 0x001FFF
 ..  ..  ..
```

Every process running in the memory uses the memory in a manor as if it is the only program running. The MMU translates all addresses used by the application code to physical addresses in the memory. Neither application code nor CPU must take care of this (Figure

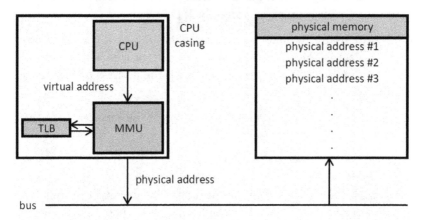

CPU: Central Processing Unit
MMU: Memory Management Unit
TLB: Translation lookaside buffer
Figure 6.1: MMU functionality

6.1).

This technique brings along a lot of security because is isolates all processes from each other. No process but the OS kernel is able to read or write information in the address space of another process. If a process tries to access memory that isn't allocated by the MMU, the MMU forces an interrupt and the process is killed by the kernel.

This doesn't imply that a process cannot do no harm to itself! The MMU doesn't recognize improper access to allocated memory. A process can for instance write data beyond the memory of one of its variables just filling vital other data with nonsense. The consequences of such events are hardly predictable.

The process itself keeps track of its stack usage. If the reserved amount is not sufficient, it asks the OS for more space automatically. Heap space can be demanded by the application programmer and must be given back to OS when no longer needed.

The data transfer between processes can now easily be understood. The requesting process prepares the request data in its RAM and loads the start address of the data into a register. The kernel is now able to access the request data set and do some checks whether the data structure was prepared correctly. It then can

- temporarily map the request data along with some control data to the address space of the service which now can handle the request when started with the address of the data in one register, or

- copy the data to the address space of the service which then can proceed accordingly.

The way back is done in the same way.

Exercise. Investigate both possibilities with regard to simplicity and security. A process, even the kernel and other OS processes, shouldn't have to know to much of the internals of other processes, and malicious programming of one process shouldn't result in failures of the service process. Try to set up a satisfactory scheme.

6.4   Swapping

Today, the computers come most often with enough RAM to hold all processes (2-4 GB, sometimes more), but it may happen that an application is loaded demanding more memory than available.

To deal with such events the operating system can swap processes being seldom used to the hard disk just freeing the RAM space for the new process.

If the swap process is needed again, it is reloaded to the RAM and executed. If the memory consuming application hasn't finished yet, another idle process is possibly swapped to the disk. Because disk operation is a slow process compared with RAM access, swap operations can painfully slow down the system.

Memory consuming processes can be swapped partly themselves. Image manipulation often consumes very large amounts of space, and the operating system may decide to swap parts of the allocated heap to the disk. Because the operating system doesn't know what the image manipulation program will do next, this may result in many swap operations nearly freezing the whole application. If the programmer knows of the memory appetite of his application, the better strategy is to configure the maximum of space demanded by the application, and let the application temporarily export excess data itself.

A memory leak emerges when the programmer forgets to free allocated heap data. If the application runs for a long time, new memory is eventually allocated to an amount that the operating system begins to swap memory parts which are, however, never used again. This results in a growth of the swapping area on the disk, eventually filling all the disk space available.

Swapping can be done to a file in the normal file system or to a special partition, which can be used for further improvements (see chapter 6.5).

Exercise and historical remark. The early PC work stations came with only about 600 kB of RAM space for OS, application, and data. Bigger applications were, therefore, organized to overlays: the code of functions never calling each other were swapped. To minimize time losses the functions had to be grouped in one module so that alternately called function were placed in one overlay. Taking into consideration the depth of function calls (function calls function calls function ...) function were organized sometimes in five or more overlay layers, each four or more modules in the broad.

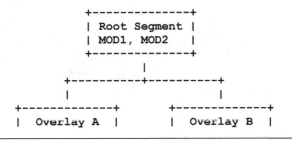

```
              +---------------+
              | Root Segment  |
              | MOD1, MOD2    |
              +---------------+
                      |
          +-----------+-----------+
          |                       |
  +---------------+       +---------------+
  |  Overlay A    |       |  Overlay B    |
```

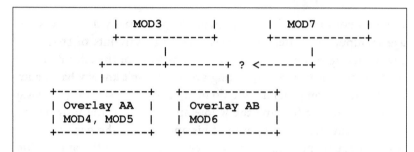

The structure could be a tree structure or layer structure. Try to find out how an algorithm for automated distribution of functions to the overlays may work.

6.5   File System

The operating system has to manage perhaps 200 processes stored in the RAM but hundreds of thousands of applications and data files in the disk. A simple list certainly doesn't fit the situation. The data on the disk have to be organized in another way to get fast access to data.

Although all file systems look similar to the user, each has its own strategy to deal with certain problems. Therefore, we can only give a general survey here.

- ReiserFS: Linux
- ext3/ext4: Linux
- btrfs: Linux
- XFS: Linux und IRIX
- JFS/JFS2: Linux, AIX und OS/2
- NTFS: Microsoft Windows
- HFS+: Mac OS X
- advfs: Tru64 UNIX
- BeFS: BeOS
- FFS: BSD
- SFS (SmartFilesystem), PFS (Professional-File-System): Amiga
- VxFS: AIX, HP-UX, Linux und Solaris

Figure 6.2: short selection of file systems

6.5.1   General Organization

The space on the disk is most often organized in several indexing and data areas. The organization has some retroactive effects on the user visible data organization, but this is hided transparently from the user who hardly recognizes differences between file systems. In the following we will restrict ourselves to the user view and some general problems.

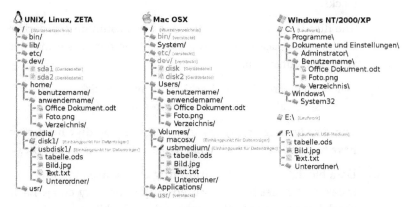

Figure 6.3: tree structure of file systems

The files (=logical associated data blocks) on the disk are organized in directories which are special files containing a sorted list of names and addresses where the corresponding data can be found (Figure 6.3). Entries in a directory may be data or application files or directories again, resulting in a tree structure organization. Each directory can hold arbitrary amounts of entries. Such a tree organization allows for

- rapid retrieval of files by the user, and

- rapid insertion of new data.

Search algorithms in simple sorted lists are of order $O(\log(n))$, but man doesn't look at large lists like a machine and searching for him is more like $O(n)$. Altering simple lists is of order $O(n)$ for machines too. In sorted trees searching for man is far easier, and machine altering is also better and of the order $O(\log(n))$.

Large files, either directories or data files, may require more than one data block on the disk. To deal with large blocks several strategies are possible:

a) All data blocks are sequentially arranged to one super block.

   The advantage of this arrangement is a fast and simple access because the disk heads have not to move much between tracks.

   The disadvantage on the other hand is a common reordering of the disk space to keep the blocks together which may be very time consuming.

b) Data blocks are allocated arbitrarily on the disk and the indexes of the allocated block are stored in special index lists.

   The disadvantage of a) is turned off, but the disk head may have to do a lot of movements to collect the data of one file.

c) Data blocks are allocated arbitrarily on the disk, but only the index of the first block is stored in the directory entry. Each block has a pointer to the next block (linked list).

Strategy c) was used in early file system with only small amounts of space compared to today disks. Strategy b) is better suited for large disk spaces and large files. It allows also for a partial super block building towards a) because the central indexing of all blocks allow for an easy rearranging of the blocks at idle times.

Many file systems tend to become slow because of many fragmented files. Defragmentation is a regularly maintenance procedure in some systems. Others use distribution strategies of the files and do without defragmentation, but this works only well when the disk has large amounts of free space. Statistical methods of the disk controller to read data ahead of demands from the CPU have already been mentioned.

Exercise. During installation of an OS is often recommended to create separate partitions for applications and data file. What may be the impact of this strategy with respect to fragmentation?

6.5.2   File System Specials

Sometimes it is desirable to find a file in more than one directory or to use it with an alias. Most file systems allow links allowing exactly this. The operating system keeps track of updates of the originals and informs applications using the link by signals.

A signal is a special flag/bit set in the operating system. An application can

- ask the operating system via a special interrupt function whether a signal is pending, or

- tell the operating system the address of a special signal processing function which is activated by the OS instead of the normal program course when a signal is pending.

The same applies to files that are attached by multiple applications. An application may demand exclusive access to a file. Other applications are then excluded from write operations and perhaps read operations, too. If multiple file access is allowed, the operating system signals alterations to the other users which then can load the updated file version.

Because the file system provides a very easy handling for the user, the principles are extended to other data sources or drains. If the files are separated on several disk partitions, the OS partition can mount complete partitions as directories. The real physical source is hided from the user who just opens another directory containing files and directories.

Communication between applications can be organized in pipes which are unidirectional in most cases. Keyboard input to or display out from an application can be thought of as pipe, but sending or receiving data from another active application is also possible. Pipes are handled like files, only provided with special opening and closing procedures to synchronize the processes. Pipe communication may be coupled with signaling to make the work flow more effective. The same principle applies to data exchange with external devices.

6.5.3   All Rights reserved

A very important aspect of security is the decision who is allowed to attach data or run applications. In the Linux operating system each file is marked with several property bits:

```
drwxrwxr-x    3 user user    .gEDA
drwx------    4 user user    .gegl-0.0
drwxr-xr-x   22 user user    .gimp-2.6
drwxr-xr-x   24 user user    .gimp-2.8
-rw-r-----    1 user user    .gksu.lock
drwx------    4 user user    .gnome2
drwx------    2 user user    .gnome2_private
drwx------    2 user root    .gnome-desktop
drwx------    4 user user    .gnupg
drwx------    2 user user    .gphoto
drwxrwxr-x    2 user user    .gstreamer-0.10
```

Every user on a system – at least two, namely the operating system and the owner – get a special user id. Some OS processes have their own user. If somebody wants to get access to a system, he has to log in with his name and a special password and access is granted under control of his user id.

Every user can belong to one or multiple groups which allow right management on a larger scale.

Every file – directory, application, or data file – is marked with the user id of the user who created the file, and the group the user was attached to during creation (in the above example user and group are named 'user').

As can be observed, every file has at least 10 property bits grouped into 1 – 3 – 3 – 3 bit groups. The first bit or bit group, in the example marked 'd', is the directory property. If set, the file is a directory. This property can, naturally, not be changed. The three following group mark

- **User rights.** Usually the owner can read from and write to a file. The owner may restrict his rights for security reasons.

- **Group rights.** Other users sharing the given group with the owner can use these rights.

- **General rights.** The last group describes rights usable by all other users of the system.

Each group defines three rights, namely

- **Readable.** If this bit is set, the user may read the file. If for example, a directory isn't marked with the read bit the user only can see the directory name, but cannot enter the directory to get a list of the files contained. The same applies to all other files.

- **Writable.** Only with this right the content of a file can be altered. If for example, a file is marked as 'writable', the content can be altered. This holds also if the home directory of the file is not marked 'writable', but a new file in this directory cannot be created (or an old one deleted).

- **Executable.** Only files marked as 'executable' can be executed as an application. This mark must in most cases be applied in a special step and is an important security action.

The security impact of the 'executable' mark is evident: a program loaded from external sources cannot be executed before altering the mark, especially it cannot execute itself without special allowance form the user. Some operating systems without this security measure show extreme vulnerability to all sorts of malware.

To alter the marks, the right to write must be present. Most application directories belong to the operating system, and to install new installations administrator rights are necessary. Because special passwords are needed to get these rights, the systems are also protected from a lot of violations of security policies of irresponsible users.

Exercise. If you have access to a computer with another OS than Linux, compare the right systems and evaluate the relative security.

6.5.4   Guarding the Rights

To guard the rights is an easy job for the operating system. The login process of a user is executed with administrator or "root" rights because this process belongs to the OS and only waits for a user to log in. After checking the user data which is possible because "root" rights grant access to everything, the process is cloned in memory, one clone being the parent, the other the child. The parent may continue to wait for other users to log in, but has at least to wait until the child terminates before he ends himself.

The child process now changes the actual directory position to the home directory of the user, loads perhaps further user data and eventually drops the rights to user rights. Now the clone can only do what is allowed to the user.

Upgrading to administrator level again or "sidegrading" to another user's rights is only possible when the administrator password is known. This keeps unauthorized users out of critical zones of the file system.

Every application started by the user – office suites, image manipulation, email agents – is executed as a child process of the first user process or another running user process and, therefore, is also executed with user rights. The same application started in another terminal of another user has the rights of that user and may attach completely different files.

> **Exercise.** When shutting down a user session the execution doesn't stop abruptly but the open windows of running applications are closed one after the other. Explain that from the discussed principles.

6.5.5   Journaling

Because disk I/O is a slow operation – the speed is scaled down from cache access via RAM access and SATA access (the title of the serial data bus between main board and disk controller) to physical disk

I/O – the operating system may apply a strategy not to execute all steps at once. Data may be stored at some location with faster access and the full execution is delayed until some idle time. But this may cause problems when the normal system operation is disturbed, for example, by power failure.

Similar problems may arise when bigger files have to be handled or blocks on the disk have to be rearranged. And it is not only power failure which can do harm: even in sophisticated systems situations may arise when the user is forced to a hard reset or internal states run into in unmanaged error.

Many file systems have a book keeper to cope with this. The operations to execute are immediately noted in a special section of the disk, and the successfully termination is noted, too. If a severe error prevents the proper execution of the chain, the system can later on after a restart repair the missing parts of the chain.

In most cases modern file systems don't need to recover from a power failure, but terminate all open activities. In earlier OS versions the addressing scheme of the file system was often heavily damaged by such drastic events and not all files could be recovered properly (a check is, however, done by each OS from time to time).

Because execution chains are completely carried out after some time, the system has to look from time to time which parts of the journal have to be erased.

Exercise. Describe a workflow for fast storing application data from RAM to the swap partition, followed by a slower process transferring the data to the file system on the main partition block by block. Do the same for a file copy operation. Analise the conditions under which errors may occur.

6.5.6   I/O Examples

As an example, we assume that an application wants to read data from
the disk. The first operation is to "open the file". The complete file-
name including all directory names which can look like

```
/usr/include/c++/4.6/bits/fstream.tcc
```

is copied to a special memory address which is then transferred to the
file system part of the operating system by a special interrupt. The directories in the path sequences are separated by "/". If the file is available, it is attached to the application.

Attaching a resource to an application can be done in two ways:

a) A complete data structure necessary to describe the resource
    is allocated in the memory space of the application. The ad-
    dress is passed to the operating system in one register and
    the operating system can determine the physical address
    from the MMU virtual table.

b) The data structure of the resource is allocated in the memory
    space of the driver. The application only gets a handle to the
    resource, that is a number specifying the resource.

Method a) has the advantage that less memory is allocated for the
driver. The disadvantage is the ability of the application to alter the
resource data which the driver operates on. The application may try
to get access to data it has no rights for.

This can not happen in method b) because only the handle is available to the application which can, however, submit the handle to another application which then has access to the resource. Sometimes
this is wanted, sometimes this is forbidden, and the operating system
may attach further properties to handles (the normal strategy allows
only child processes to use handles).

In method b) it is also easier to synchronize the state of the file attached to different applications, but the driver has to keep track of
the lifetime of the owner process. He has to release the resource
when the process terminates.

When data are read from the disk, there are also two possible mechanisms to realize that:

a) The application allocates memory for the data and sends the address to the operating system via an interrupt call.

    The operating system inserts the memory temporarily to the disk driver via the MMU tables, giving it the address in a CPU registers. On termination of the driver the memory is transferred back to the calling application.

b) The disk driver allocates the data in his memory space giving the operating system the address after termination. The operating system allocates the memory in the address space of the application, and it is to the application to free it after usage.

Both methods seem to be in usage, but what exactly happens in the kernels of the different operating systems is somewhat mysterious, because only some are open source and can be studied in detail.

6.6   Threads

Processes have completely different logical address spaces and can, therefore, not interfere with each other. Because of the high efficiency of the modern hardware, especially the multi kernel CPUs, calculations in one application can also be done in parallel if the algorithm allows for parallel calculation.

As a somewhat silly example one may think of a window telling the user to be more patient during some not interruptible calculations when he hits the keyboard again, instead of typing ahead something blindly. As a more suitable example many image manipulation algorithms can be parallelized and multi CPUs can work at the same time (now really the same time) at one picture.

To manage this processes in processes, named threads, have to be put up. Threading is done in the following way:

•   The address space of the program area and the heap area are attached to several processes.

- Each thread has its own stack somewhere memory. The stacks don't interfere, but a pointer of a local variable of a thread may be transferred to another thread to give him access to the variable.

To test the positions of the stack areas it is sufficient to print out the address of a local variable.

```
size_t i;
printf("Thread %d %lx\n",j,&i);

Master 7fffc40ef7f0
Thread 0 7f6f088fae58
Thread 1 7f6f080f9e58
Thread 2 7f6f078f8e58
Thread 3 7f6f070f7e58
Thread 4 7f6f068f6e58
```

The distance of the different stacks in this example is about 8 MB. Following these strategies not much has to be done in the compilers. The stack mechanism is the same as in linear programs, and the code is shared by all threads. Only the operating system has to keep track of the table of active threads and to switch between them by switching between the different stacks. The dependencies of processes – parent and children – apply also to threads.

Because all threads use the same program and head space, some carefulness has to be spend for synchronization:

- If a critical operation in the memory takes several commands, a thread must be able to lock other threads from interrupting it during that operation.

  After having terminated the critical section the lock has to be deleted.

```
lock('Section1');
.. .. ..               // critical
unlock('Section1');
```

Other threads have to wait until the lock is erased before entering the section themselves:

```
wait_lock('Section1');
.. .. ..               // critical
```

- If a thread needs another thread to realize some calculations before it can come in, the thread must be able to signalize an idle condition to avoid wast of calculation time.

```
set_wait('cond1');
.. .. ..                    // critical
```

In response a thread must be able to signalize that he has finished certain operations so that other threads can come in.

```
release_cond('cond1');
```

The code in this section is not taken from a programming language but only provided to visualize the method. The image is, however, far to simple. If a thread checks, whether a certain lock was set, he would probably set himself a lock when entering the section. The locking mechanism must avert situations in which a lock condition is set between the check and the set operation, because then two threads are working in the critical section producing some nonsense.

If a condition is set, the thread probably must control whether another thread has cared about the condition, before he himself enters a critical or condition section again.

At least circular locks must be averted. This can happen when a thread ought to release a lock but the unlock event takes place in a critical region and the thread doesn't get to this position because he is locked by another process. If this process is in the same situation – the unlock event cannot be reached before a lock situation before – and the responsible thread is the first one, the show ends here. The situation can be even more complicated when more threads play this game in a circle. But we must admit that most of these situations occur, because the programmer has made some essential flaws.

Effective threading needs some support by the operating system. Threads are part of the programming language only in a few languages, but all languages provide thread libraries, so we can say threading is a standard operation method today. But although threading is not really new, a lot of work is still to be done. Multiple CPU kernels allow, in principle, parallelizing on the scale of a few commands (see chapter 2.1.1). A for loop can, for example, be split in many single blocks under certain circumstances. This can be regarded as some kind of threading, but the concepts are not very far developed.

Exercise. A warehouse (the shared data) is filled by track A (the first thread) with one box on each visit, another track B (the second thread) removes three boxes on each visit but doing nothing if less than three boxes are in the warehouse. Only one truck can enter the warehouse and has to wait if the other is inside. If track B finds not enough boxes in the warehouse, he does not need to enter the warehouse again until truck A has unloaded new boxes. Describe these states using locking etc.

6.7   Virtualization

As we already mentioned, modern server mainboards may include a lot of CPU kernels, and several mainboards may be plugged together by a connection bus to an even higher integrated system. But the tasks of an operating system don't scale to such number. Apart from some very special operating systems for super computers the scaling stops at 16 oder 32 kernels, and the 1-2 TB of RAM on a modern server mainboard may also be not very meaningful.

For that reason a further software layer – the virtualization layer – is placed between hardware and operating system. It cuts an specified amount of "logical hardware" from the available physical hardware und presents this portion to an operating system. You may think of a virtualization system as a reduced operating system whose clients are full operating systems.

We don't go into the details on this topic. Forinstance you have already heard of VirtualBox or other tools, which allow to operate other operating systems inside the native operating system of your computer, so you can try it yourself. The techniques are very effecive: the loss is between 2-10% compared to an operating system working on native hardware.

7 Network and Security

Modern computers are unthinkable without a network connection. The network can be connected by wired lan technology, wireless lan technology, usb lan connection, mobile phones, and more. To enable all kind of machines from manufactures all over the world to communicate with each other universal communication protocols are necessary, the most important being the protocols of the TCP/IP family.

The connection of computers by networks bring along not only joy, but also some trouble. Not all players in the net are honest. And they have direct access to other computers via the network. Networks are a preferred target of hackers (and intelligence) to get access to private data like credit card accounts, bank accounts, or customer's data. The damage caused to the public by compromised data is in the order of several billion US-$ per year solely in the US. Therefore, every computer user has to perform some safety measures in order not to be unpleasantly surprised. That's why we added "Security" to the heading of this chapter.

We will do this in the following manor: we begin with a very short insight in lower internet protocols ("what everyone should know about TCP/IP"), proceed to social engineering ("what everyone should know about stupidity") and computer security ("what everyone should know about his laptop") and end with some remarks on internet working ("what everyone should know how to do it wrong"). Security is included as a smaller or larger part of each lesson.

7.1   TCP/IP Networking

A protocol is a detailed definition of how a specified amount of information should be transmitted. The definitions for the TCP/IP family are collected in a paper library named "Request for Comments", short

RFC, which can be accessed via the internet. If the reader, for example, wants to know how to communicate with the pop3 mail server of his provider without usage of a local mail agent, he can load RFC1939 and look for the details. But pay attention if you do so. After a slowly begin in the 1990 the RFC numbers of new protocols now operate in the range of 6,000, and elder versions of a protocol are not deleted. RFC1939 obsoletes for instance RFC1725, and it may happen that not all communication details are met if you refer to an obsolete version. Because the protocols are ordered by date, not by subject, a search operation is necessary to find the informations.

7.1.1   The lower Layers

If we think a little about different protocols like sending and receiving emails, web browsing, file transfer, or internet telephone – we must

OSI Model			
	Data unit	Layer	Function
Host layers	Data	7. Application	Network process to application
		6. Presentation	Data representation, encryption and decryption, convert machine dependent data to machine independent data
		5. Session	Interhost communication, managing sessions between applications
	Segments	4. Transport	Reliable delivery of packets between points on a network.
Media layers	Packet/Datagram	3. Network	Addressing, routing and (not necessarily reliable) delivery of datagrams between points on a network.
	Bit/Frame	2. Data link	A reliable direct point-to-point data connection.
	Bit	1. Physical	A (not necessarily reliable) direct point-to-point data connection.

Figure 7.1: OSI layer model

not be familiar with the details because we only draw logical conclusions – there are some tasks like finding a route between source and destination which appear in every protocol. It is a good idea to reuse software already written for such purposes instead of inventing it over and over again. A detailed analysis let the engineers arrange the reappearing parts in so called protocol layers (Figure 7.1). Each layer has a specific function, and it has to do its job transparent to the layer above, and below. Let's explain the model in short.

Starting with the data link layer in Figure 7.1 which is in home networks often represented by the ethernet protocol, the protocols have to transport the data from one physical network connection port to another one which is directly connected to the first by wire, wireless lan, or usb. Necessary to do the job is only the knowledge of the physical addresses of the connection ports (the MAC address, Figure 7.2). The hardware device is able to recognize its own address in the frame and takes only frames with this address to further processing. Included in the ethernet protocol is support for data integrity. But the layer definitions have neither to bother about how the signals are coded electrically on the wire nor what information is transported in the data section and how the information is coded.

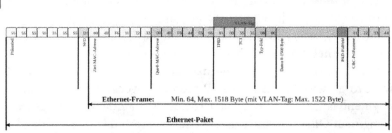

Figure 7.2: ethernet frame

Exercise. The ethernet protocol has a so called preambel. Compare it and the CRC information to the organization of hard disk data and identify similarities.

The next layer, the link layer, is responsible to route datagrams between machines that are not necessary directly connected to each other. The mentioned MAC address only describes the hardware device, the computer itself owns one or more logical addresses – the IP address – to identify the machine in the internet. In version 4 of the protocol the IP address is (only) 32 bits wide which is too small to give each computer in the world an individual address, but the next version 6 can achieve that with 128 bits per address.

0–3	4–7	8–11	12–15	16–18	19–23	24–27	28–31
Version	IHL	Type of Service		Gesamtlänge			
Identifikation				Flags	Fragment Offset		
TTL		Protokoll		Header-Prüfsumme			
Quell-IP-Adresse							
Ziel-IP-Adresse							
evtl. Optionen ...							

Figure 7.3: IP protocol frame

The IP addresses are only 1/3 of the header, therefore, we can suppose that there are a lot more things to manage. One thing to manage is fragmentation: the ethernet frame only transports a maximum of about 1,500 bytes, and most application data blocks are much larger. Each ethernet data frame has to contain an IP header because without the information in this header the software layer doesn't know what to do with the data. The IP protocol layer is, therefore, able to fragment large application data (fields "Gesamtlänge", "Flags", and "Fragment Offset" in the header) and to reassemble them at the destination.

The protocol further takes into account fast and slow transport paths between source and destination which may result in multiple data blocks received simultaneously. The "Identifikation" field allows to assign the incoming fragments to the right data block.

The field "TTL" is responsible for life time control. It cannot be guaranteed that a frame arrives at the destination, and misrouted fragments are erased from the network after some defined time.

The IP protocol is only responsible for routing the data, but not for interpreting them at the destination. The field "Type of Service" tells the layer software which next higher layer is the recipient on the system.

Exercise. MAC address as the physical address and IP address as the logical address must be linked. The protocol doing that allows for deception: a hacker (Mallory, Figure 7.4) can play the role of a man-in-the-middle and signal to Bob that she is Alice and vice versa. Search for detail in the web using the keyword "ARP spoofing".

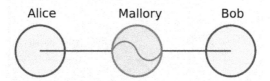

Figure 7.4: man in the middle

The next layer protocol may be transmission control protocol TCP above the IP layer. It establishes two further logical address numbers, the port numbers, which specify the applications on the systems communicating with each other (Figure 7.5). The combination of the four numbers IP:port-port:IP

Client-System	Server-system
IP-Adress:Port	IP-Adress:Port
137.129.1.117:3347	87.102.88.7:80
114.197.2.107:2121	87.102.88.7:80

is called a socket and is a unique identifier for one connection between two applications.

To understand that in detail we have to introduce the client-server-concept. If a communication is to take place, one partner – the client – has to initiate it, the other – the server – must be ready to react on this. Think of a telephone call to get an impression of the principle: you as the caller are the client, the person you are calling is the server. In order to get a connection to the desired person you have to know her number. That is also true for internet connectivity: a mail server has a RFC defined port number, and you can connect to an arbitrary mail server by using its IP address and the official port number for servers of that type. Some port number are, therefore, reserved for server processes. The client, however, may use any port that is not in use. The socket part of the server can, therefore, be used in many connections, as is displayed in the above socket table.

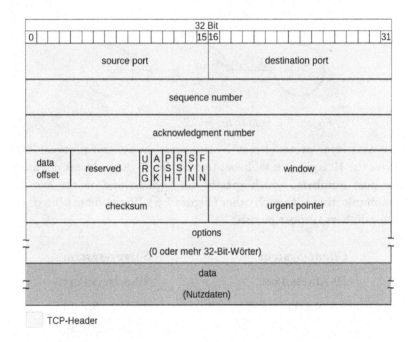

Figure 7.5: TCP header

The TCP header not only specifies the port numbers but simulates something like a telephone line. All data blocks are numbered (fields "sequence number" and "acknowledgement number") in order to guarantee the sequence of the data blocks, the correct transmission, and the persistence of connection during idle times. Establishing a persistent connection over a network only transmitting single data blocks is a little bit tricky and the following Figure 7.6 shall give you an impression of what's going on:

Above the TCP layer different application protocols appear, some of which are similar in construction to the lower layer protocols, some are text driven like a conversation between man. We can't go into the

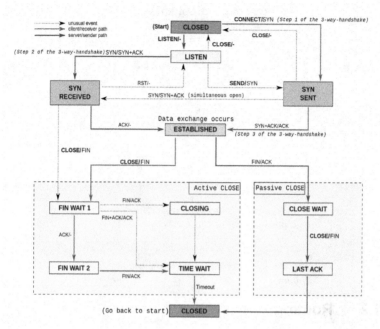

Figure 7.6: TCP handshaking

details here, but the layers are rather crowded with different protocol suites (Figure 7.7).

To sum all up, (nearly) each protocol comes with its own header part followed by the data. The layers are nested like onion peels: the ethernet frame starts with its own header and the first bytes of the data part in each ethernet frame contain an IP header. The data section of the IP header contains a TCP header, but only once for a complete block. If the IP block is fragmented, the TCP header is not repeated in each fragment. The TCP header is, however, followed by the application layer headers, and at least also some data are transferred. If other protocol combinations are necessary to do the job, the principle is to be applied accordingly.

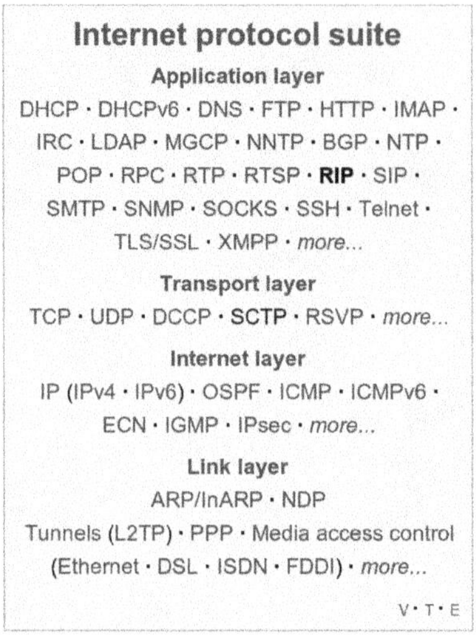

> **Internet protocol suite**
>
> **Application layer**
> DHCP · DHCPv6 · DNS · FTP · HTTP · IMAP ·
> IRC · LDAP · MGCP · NNTP · BGP · NTP ·
> POP · RPC · RTP · RTSP · **RIP** · SIP ·
> SMTP · SNMP · SOCKS · SSH · Telnet ·
> TLS/SSL · XMPP · *more...*
>
> **Transport layer**
> TCP · UDP · DCCP · **SCTP** · RSVP · *more...*
>
> **Internet layer**
> IP (IPv4 · IPv6) · OSPF · ICMP · ICMPv6 ·
> ECN · IGMP · IPsec · *more...*
>
> **Link layer**
> ARP/InARP · NDP
> Tunnels (L2TP) · PPP · Media access control
> (Ethernet · DSL · ISDN · FDDI) · *more...*
>
> V · T · E

Figure 7.7: protocols in the different layers.

7.1.2 Routing

Because the IPv4 address range is rather small, and additionally for security reasons, some addresses are not universal, but can be used in multiple local lans. The IP range 192.168.x.x is an example of local usable IP addresses. One single local lan (for example your own home network) using only this range may contain up to 65,000 computers which reliefs the internet of strain when applied even to large companies.

For the communication with an internet server, however, an official internet IP is necessary. The door of a local lan to the internet is a router which maps the inner address to outer addresses. A router has at least two network connections, one to the local lan with a local IP adsress, and a second one to the internet with an official internet IP address.

When the IP layer of a work station has to transmit data to a destination, it compares the address to a local scheme:

```
dest-ip AND cut-mask =?= local-mask
```

If the check fits the local mask, the recipient is in the local lan and the message is directly send to the MAC address of the recipient. If the check fails, the recipient is somewhere in the internet (or another not directly connected segment of the local netwerk) and the datagram is sent using the MAC address of the router as destination.

> **Exercise.** You already know of all these terms if you have a com-puter with internet access at home. Figure out all details about "network mask" and "gateway" from internet information sources and explain in detail to a comrade (who should behave a little im-becile to make sure that the explanations are really complete and understandable.

The router recognizes on receiving the datagram that he is not meant because it doesn't contain its IP address. The router changes the inner source IP to its own outer universal IP address and perhaps also changes the port address if it is already in use at the outer side (net-work address translation NAT). The modified data are send to the destination. The router keeps a table of these address translations to route the answer back to the inner computer (Figure 7.8 and Figure

lokales Netz (LAN)		Router	öffentliches Netz (WAN)	
Quelle	**Ziel**		**Quelle**	**Ziel**
192.168.0.2:4701	170.0.0.1:80	=====	**205.0.0.2:6787**	170.0.0.1:80
192.168.0.3:5387	170.0.0.1:80	= =====>	**205.0.0.2:8709**	170.0.0.1:80
192.168.0.4:1001	170.0.0.1:23	**NAT**	**205.0.0.2:4806**	170.0.0.1:23

Figure 7.8: outgoing NAT

7.9)

The server now communicates formally with the router, not with the inner client. When an answer arrives the router looks up its address table and translates the destination address to the local address leav-ing the rest to the client.

öffentliches Netz (WAN)		Router	lokales Netz (LAN)	
Quelle	Ziel		Quelle	Ziel
170.0.0.1:1001	171.4.2.1:80	===== =	170.0.0.1:1001	192.168.0.2:80
170.0.0.1:1001	171.4.2.1:22	=====>	170.0.0.1:1001	192.168.0.3:22
170.0.0.1:1001	171.4.2.1:81	NAT	170.0.0.1:1001	192.168.0.3:81

Figure 7.9: incoming NAT

The (security) advantage of address translation is that only datagrams are able to enter the local lan that are requested by local clients. Other datagrams don't have an entry in the NAT table of the router and are discarded. On the other hand, only client systems can connect to outer systems. The router may have a persistent table entry for a server port and the send all incoming messages on that port to a server inside, but as the router has only one official internet IP address and the server processes have to be reachable on certain port numbers only single servers can be routed through a NAT router.

I have a high value placed on NAT, because I want to make you familiar with one of the central security features, but most routers in homogeneous lan environments don't perform NAT operations. Routers completely inside a local lan or the internet don't change the socket informations, but they have to finger out whom to send the message next, too. To connect a client in the US to a server in Europe take about 15-20 routers in between. But to discuss that is beyond out scope.

7.1.3   Domain Name Service

We only mentioned IP addresses so far. IP addresses have the disadvantage that they are poorly memorized by man. A better idea are ordinary names which are mapped by the domain name service DNS to IP addresses. The user enters the name and the machine internally translates to IP addresses:

```
www.google.de   --- DNS --->   173.194.69.94
```

The names are structured similar to directory trees, the parts separated by points. The extension ".de" indicates the managing organization DENIC which maps the name to IP addresses and has further information about the holder of the name. The middle part identifies an organization, and further starting parts may differentiate between different servers or server applications.

The DNS brings along some other advantages:

- The server may be moved to other IP addresses without the need to learn other addresses for the user.

- Very strong occupied organizations like google may use several servers even in different countries with different IP addresses. The DNS protocol is able to transmit several IP addresses belonging to one name.

- Some well known organizations use different names, perhaps with differing managing organizations, to reach all customers. All names are mapped to the same address set.

- Private person may want to offer their own internet page with a special name. Web hosters can store different web pages with different names using only one single IP address.

DNS is part of the information a computer to internet <u>must</u> have. You probably know this from attaching your computer to the internet. Some fraud is possible from

- transmitting false IP resolution from malicious DNS servers or

- installing domains with similar, but often mistyped names to good servers by hackers.

7.1.4   Emails

Nearly everyone owns at least one email account to send and receive electronic messages. The protocols are rather simple:

- **SMTP** or simple mail transfer protocol is used to send mails to a recipient.

- **POP3** or post office protocol version 3 is used to transfer email from a server to a local mail agent like Thunderbird.

- **IMAP** is used to organize the emails on a server only reading them in a browser.

Emails are one of the preferred targets of intelligence. Compared to normal mail emails are similar to post cards: the content isn't secured and everybody having access to the network can read it. Nonetheless the most private things are transmitted by emails.

I know of a business transaction between a Chinese and a German company in which goods were ordered and invoices sent – with the result that both, goods and money, vanished forever. A clever hacker in Singapore managed to exchange the contents in both directions. The delivery address was as well forged as the bank account. Some security measures like signing the mail or encrypt them, and both companies would be much happier.

Some people think that encryption of the smtp and pop3 connection will do it. Unfortunately this is completely wrong! Only the transmission line is encrypted, but every mail router will see the content of the mail in clear. If encryption shall secure the content, it must be arranged between sender and receiver. It's not very difficult, because encryption is included in most mail agents. But that need at least three or four clicks for the user – clearly too many for most people. So we can only state here that a lot of users seem to be learning resistant because they are always very upset by bad events, but don't take any step to prevent from being harmed.

Exercise. I mentioned "signing" of emails. Try to find out what is behind the term "signature" and what is to do to sign (and encrypt) mails.

7.1.5   HTTP Server

A web side is a must today even for small businessmen, and a lot of private persons, the author included, have their own pages. Programming in this area isn't very demanding, but is very demanding. Uups, a typing error? No, it isn't, it's intention. Let's have a short look at the details:

- The first step of web page development is HTML programming. You may use a special HTML editor, but in the end you have to bother with something like this:

```
<div>
  <ul>
    <li><a href="index.php/entries/show_entry/"
                  target="_blank">dididi</a></li>
  </ul>
</div>
```

- Not colored enough? Okay, let's move to CSS:

```
body {
  background-color: #fff;
  margin: 40px;
  font: 13px/20px Arial, sans-serif;
  color: #4F5155;
}
```

- If you want to add some motion, the next trick is named JavaScript

```
function Zustand() {
  this.is_folder = true;
  this.partkey = "";
  this.edit = "";
  this.node_key = 0;
}
```

- OK, that's the client part. But what is happening on the server? Perhaps you will sell something and a server application has to be developed, perhaps using the PHP skript language:

```
class Entries extends CI_Controller{
  public function __construct(){
    parent::__construct();
```

```
}
```

- Where to store the order? A database is needed:

```
SELECT DISTINCT b.key,b.is_folder
   FROM `kartei` AS a
   JOIN `kartei` AS b
      ON a.key LIKE CONCAT(b ..
```

To get all to work you have to occupy with five different programming concepts concerning two different machines. The beginning is not very demanding, and as you learn to use all concepts in small portions it may be in all in all not very demanding to get something running. The main problem is that you are not the only person to deal with your application: everyone can do something on your page, and some of these persons may not be very friendly.

To come to the point: there are are huge amounts of security holes into which you can fall. During the development you spent 100% of your time to make your application colorful and loud with about 15% of time spend for repair of accidentally misbehavior of a user. A hacker spends 100% of his time on designed misbehavior to hack your side. Who, do you think, will win the race?

In the appendix of this book you will find another book of this author concerning only server security.

7.1.6   Voice over IP

This part of the internet traffic gets more and more important because even traditional telephone companies like the German telekom offer their customers voice over IP. A short overview is therefore appropriate.

An IP telephone needs a special router to function properly which is called SIP server. On power on the telephone connects to the next SIP server, the address of which is probably provided by a DCHP initializing, and registers there to be ready. To call someone, a user simple keys in a telephone number which is send to the SIP server.

The SIP server asks a special DNS version for the address of the responsible destination SIP server. This server may, however, have information that the telephone has been registered at another SIP server, which learned from the phone data the name of the responsible SIP server, and connected this server to confirm the registering. This process is call "roaming". The logically responsible SIP server, therefore, routes the contact to the physically responsible one.

This server checks whether the destination phone is ready to accept a call and initiated ringing. If the person called picks up, both SIP servers initiate an entry in their NAT table to let the phones communication directly. Due to efficiency both telephones act as client to send data and server to receive data using a specially modified protocol.

On termination of the connection the SIP servers erase the NAT table line, and do some smalltalk to settle over tolls.

7.2   General Remarks on Security

Today, most of out life is documented on our computer: photos, documents, videos, and probably very private things like fingerprints, medical data, and so on. How secure are these data? Who can get access at them? The government, organized criminals, script kiddies?

These questions also apply to commercial data. Secret development data are stored on computers as well as customer's data like addresses or credit card data. The suspicion alone that data may have been compromised may be a reason for the customer to change his supplier.

From these questions a funny (or nasty if you want to regard it like this) arises: nearly everyone gets very excited when news like the world wide spying activities of US intelligence, not excluding US citizens themselves, are spread, but nearly nobody really cares about his situation and how to secure his data. And everyone seems to be content again on the first stupid proposal of someone being involved in the scandal himself.

The situation is even worse because computer engineers often don't care themselves. New technologies of mobile phones, networked home appliances, and even networked cars on the highways are engineered to present the best possible entertainment effect, but only minor work is done on security issues.

A few examples:

- It is possible to tap the gps data of a car by the radio or the phone port, and from these data car thieves simply get information about when a car is parked, and it can be stolen at nearly no risk.

- Because all devices in a car are connected by different networks it is in principle possible to signal by radio to some devices to produce errors, and the helpful service on the spot earns money from doing nothing or installs further techniques to steal the car later on.

- In the autonomous driving time surely coming soon where the driver really does nothing but sitting behind a more or less needles steering wheel, it is only a question of time that some terrorists drive one half of the cars on a freeway to full speed, the other fraction to full stop if the carelessness goes on like now.

- A similar development can be observed in household appliances. The energy suppliers may start in near the future your washing machine or your refrigerator when enough cheap energy is available. And your neighbor may upgrade your satin lingerie washing program to 95°C or shut down your freezer some minutes after you traveled away for your 3 week vacancy.

You don't believe that? Well, think about STUXNET, a virus the US intelligence used to sabotage Iranian nuclear facilities.

7.3   Man as Source of Insecurity

7.3.1   Social Engineering

The first thing we have to consider is deception. Internet users are forced by data thieves called phishers to reveal secrets or to pay money for nothing.

Unbelievable, but psychological true: the more indirect a contact between individuals, the more secrets are willingly presented to the opponent. Nobody will tell a civil officer even his name before having checked his identification card proofing that he really is the police officer XYZ and that has the right to ask such questions. But most person will tell a phone caller claiming to be FBI agent ABC the most private details, even critical passwords.

In Germany, for example, a harm of some 10,000,000 € was caused by giving access informations for CO_2 certificates to a caller claiming to be employee of the Ministry of Economic. The information was stolen from several companies, and if you take into consideration that only a few high level employees have access to these data, you may conclude that this stupidity was committed by senior employees, and the situation is nothing better in other countries.

Ubiquitous are mail like

```
Your bank account is locked for security reasons.
To regain access please follow the link and check
your data.
```

Although the formulation is often ridiculous (because the origin of the message may be China or Bulgaria) and your bank tells you over and over again

```
We will never, really never, and under no
circumstances provide links in our mails asking
you for account data, and will never, really
never, and under no circumstances ask you for
account information .. ..
```

there seemingly exist enough people entering the link and providing some 50 TANs to the phisher.

This applies not only to bank accounts but also to web stores and other web applications. Although the rule

> **never open a link asking for account data from email**

is well known and the fraud can be detected in most cases with minor knowledge of web technology, a lot of people seem to take no care of this even on repetition.

Another trick is to feign a big amount of money somewhere in black Africa which the user can participate in if he only clicks the link and sends some money to initiate the big transfer to his account. Mails like these circulate for more than 15 years, and they probably find their victims even today.

7.3.2   Social Networking

Private information is even made public without being asked for. Although it is very well known that data on facebook and other social networks are read by all kind of intelligence and the platforms itselves often contain severe security flaws allowing hackers to access the data, people post private photos, their addresses, and even their diary in the network. If they wonder, why their home is completely empty after only three days of a short vacancy?

Albert Einstein characterized that human behavior in his own terms:

> "The size of the universe, and the human stupidity are borderless. Admittedly, in case of the universe I am not quite sure."

7.3.3   Security Policy

The first step to better security is a security policy. Even for a private person it is worth to set up such a policy. If she has formulated some rules to follow, social engineering might not be a trap to fall in, social networks not be a source of private data for everyone.

A company's security policy is to be developed on a larger base, and it is no static thing. It is a completely other kind of thinking: instead of asking how things should work, the policy maker must ask which things are not allowed to work, and it does not matter whether they are possible in the existing scene or not. Think like a hacker!

For example: who has access to which data, who is allowed to execute what action, which action is logged? A hacker may ask himself exactly these questions to find a target for some social engineering.

But this is only one side of the coin. Most attacks on systems are insider attacks. In case of most whistle blowers forinstance the first of the above questions doesn't seem to have been answered properly: why to the hell a 23 years old private first class like Bradley Manning has a top secret level authorization, and additional how can it be possible to export several hundreds of megabytes of data without notice? The same applies to Edward Snowden and other whistle blowers.

Each coin has three sides, and so a security policy has to take into account negligence, too. Employees load private software on a company's computer, install bypasses of the network, send confidential documents with email, don't lock their work station on a lunch break, …

A security policy must take all that into account, and the people concerned with policy making must have a deep inside into the technology.

7.3.4   Passwords

The most serious problem of security are passwords. A user has to identify himself at the system by typing in a password, and if it is correct, access is granted. But a security chain like any other chain is only as strong as the weakest member. 4.096 bit RSA security, and 256 bit AES security are worthless if the password is the name or birthday of the girl friend of the user. The problem is not easily to be solved, because a 130 bit password looks like this:

```
3oDfSXpbIPt6evZYtHa8bT   (only characters+numbers)
jPfsYC0)-UKFQY&Rx&_A (all printable characters)
```

Who is able to remember password like these? And who can do that for some 40-50 passwords because every account should have its own access codes, and if we buy things in Internet shops, we will have a lot of different account after some time?

Okay, 130 bits are a lot, 80 bits may be enough according to modern technologies, and even if 64 bit keys are tried out in a few hours of a brute force attack, who will invest in such an attack to read your private mail? But the main problem remains especially on company level. Some help is provided by password safes, therefore, a user has only to remember one large password, but he has to do so.

7.4   Computer Security

How secure is your computer? Who can access data on your computer or damage data? And last not least: have you access to your own data in case of an accident? This is partly a question of technology, partly a question of behavior.

7.4.1   Malware

Damage is done to your computer by malicious software (shortly malware) and malware is often feed into the computer by a careless user.

- **Viruses** are small individual programs on USB sticks, CDs, or diskettes. When the devices are attached to the computer, the programs are activated and loaded to the hard disk where it splits into a malicious executive, new infective parts, which can be transported to other systems by use of USB sticks and so on.

The viruses itself can be harmless only consuming execution time or very dangerous damaging the whole contents of the disk or encrypt the disk followed by some extortion to get access to the data again.

An example for a harmful "harmless" virus may have experienced some readers themselves. A few years ago an electrical power black out affected wide parts of the eastern US. The suspected reason was a virus only consuming time on the systems controlling the energy flow. The systems were provided with an unsuited operating system for technical purposes and additionally connected to the Internet. Eventually the software wasn't able to execute the controlling functions at the appropriate speed, and the hardware reacted rigorously on the overload.

- **Worms** are malware attached to emails. Normally they do not activate themselves but the user has to to. They often export private information from the infected system to some hacker sides.

- **Troians** are applications that split into a useful and a malicious part. The user himself loads them actively on his system, because he want to use the useful part, not knowing of the malicious one.

  The malicious parts of these applications are often very complex, because the intruder must not take care of the amount of code. Some of these programs provide complete control over the infected system to the hacker; the user only can do what the hacker allows him to do.

The defense line against such attacks are virus scanners (or an appropriate operating system which is mostly immune against such attacks). They look for software patterns of known malware and in case of detection remove the malware and warn the user. Of course, these programs can only look for known malware. If the hackers implement new tricks it takes some time for the security providers to detect it and provide their users with new versions of scanners.

The security applications often can do more:

- They can observe the network traffic for unusual ports and block the ports,

- observe the contents of the traffic for private data and erase the private data before sending, or

- observe which software tries to use network connections, and block the connection if they are not allowed to to so.

But all this needs configuration, and the normal user often neither has the knowledge nor the time nor even the interest to occupy therewith.

It is striking that the vulnerability for malware concerns mainly one operating system which even in its newest version 8 release in 2012 doesn't contain all security features other systems contain since their early versions since 1969. I led it to the philosophers to think about the question why users get very excited about security flows, but refuse in the 25th year now to change to another operating system containing only fractions of vulnerabilities.

7.4.2   Data Security

Data security on your computer system has two faces:

- Nobody should be able to steal data.
- No data should be lost by accident.

Let's begin with the second task: the life time of a hard disk is finite and the end come often very suddenly. Data recovery from a crashed disk is partly possible but very expensive. Do you have an actual backup of your data when a crash occurs?

A RAID 2 mirror disk may help, because if one disk crashes the content of the second is intact. A regular backup has the advantage that elder versions of files are also available when needed. And a mobile disk only connected to the system during the backup process may help against a flash hitting the power line and roasting the complete machine.

A modern possibility for securing data against loss is the cloud. The cloud is nothing but a trick of companies having large amounts of free disk storage and unused computing power. If you don't want your data being visible in the cloud,

- check the configuration which data are configured to be visible to others,

- check private data being encrypted before storing in the cloud,

- check who does the encryption, you or the cloud provider,

- go to church regularly to pray that all goes well.

Even if you care about a backup of your data it may be that other friendly people care too and make some backups of your data too. This care concerns mostly notebooks. The disks of notebooks often contain confidential data. Therefore, some security measures should be taken because notebooks often travel throughout the world with their owners. If a notebook is stolen somewhere, this must not have been happened by chance. One method of industrial espionage is contract theft.

The answer is encryption of the disk and usage of a hard password to get access to the disk. Encryption has to be applied on the complete disk because partial encryption lets room for data leakage. The second problem to be managed are short time intervals of absence of the owner. The notebook should be locked even for a minute of absence. Their exist some strategies to make the login after a short absence interval more comfortable but they are not wide spread.

7.4.3   Device Security

The first keyword already be mentioned earlier and to be handled here is unauthorized data import and export. Although it is a very clear security policy that only the system administration is authorized to install software, some employee thinking to be sophisticated computer specialists themselves don't care. I remember, for example, a very angry phone call one morning from a sewage treatment plant we installed the controls for that the outlet had a severe overflow during the night. A short control of the log files revealed that all three (!) main control systems have been shot down between 1 and 4 o'clock in the morning, because the personal wanted to play some computer games. Therefore, no message from the problems in the outlet could be recognized.

Negligence can do a lot of harm, and a few years later a distributed system of over 30 main control computers was infected by virus soft-ware for the same reason. It took over 4 months to clean the system completely.

Examples for the other direction of data transfer are men like Bradley Manning or Edward Snowden who "exported" several hundred mega bytes of secret data.

To prevent from such harm workstations in a lot of companies today don't have any slots for USB, CD, or diskette devices, and the cabi-nets are often locked, too.

7.5   Network Security

Networks and computers have to be prevented from unauthorized ac-cess. The first defense line of local networks are routers and several types of firewalls, of which the NAT was already mentioned.

We have also mentioned the fact that most harm is done by insiders or negligence. Therefore, not only access from outside has to be con-trolled by firewall, but access from inside to unwanted servers has also to be stopped. Concerning basic services like DNS or email the network should be configured in a way that employees not only have access to the company's servers but aren't able to use other services.

Servers themselves have to be secured. The right configuration of a server to prevent from being taken over by a hacker is an art, and in the appendix you can find another book of this author concerning with this matter.

We cannot discuss further details here, but the strategy of the secu-rity engineer always should be to achieve "maximum security". The configuration of the different system parts – routers, switches, internal servers, firewalls, and the workstations themselves – often results in the same effect. "Maximum security" means that the administrator closes a security gap on one part that is suspected to be close already on another part. "The devil is a squirrel", and if by some instance the gap is open on one part, the other jumps in.

Configuration is one part, control another. Intrusion detection systems (IDS) observe the network traffic to detect security risks or possible attacks. Today, the companies move to encrypt local network traffic by public key infrastructure which provides individual encryption for each connection to give internal eavesdroppers no chance, but this has consequences for IDS because encrypted content cannot be analyzed. Analyzing on the other hand is inevitable if the circulation of classified documents should be monitored and no document management system doing that is available.

Similar considerations affect private home networks. At least the wlan access should be secured by encryption and the user should take care not to activate encryption methods broken in minutes or seconds. These insecure methods are implemented only for downgrade compatibility with elder equipment, but too often used by unexperienced users.

And behind that, are we secure? According to Edward Snowden this is not the case, because the NSA probably can read even secured data. This sound like some conspiracy theory: is intelligence really more than 50 years ahead in knowledge and techniques than all other scientists in the world? I think Snowden can be true, but the NSA isn't as far ahead (if at all). The NSA is said to be financed by 11 billion US-$ from then federal budget, and who knows what other sources provide additionally? With that amount of money a technological protrusion is not really necessary: you can pay for being brought in.

8 Last Words

Introduction to computer science? Is this really only an introduction? Well, the claim prospected here is rather large, and you may feel that only chapters 1 – 3 are really an introduction, chapters 4 and 5 on the borderline, and chapters 6 and 7 come with to many details to be still an introduction (perhaps chapter 4 belongs already to this category).

May be I weighted some fields more than others, as I have threatened in the beginning, but yes: that's only an introduction. Some fields have only be mentioned in keywords because the background necessary to understand something is far beyond an introduction. Other topics are developed to a broader extent because I thought them easy enough to walk in even for a beginner. But even then we only scratched the surface. If you really want to become a specialist, you'll have to spend a lot of work more.

I hope that this introduction has shown you that your decision for computer science was the right one (or that it is better to think it over because you might to have to spend the rest of your working life in an area that's not really yours) and that you'll have a lot of fun in the future.

Stichwortverzeichnis

Der sichere Webserver und seine Umgebung

(in German)

Aufsetzen, Programmieren und Testen: ein Trainings-, Übungs- und Ideenbuch für den Administrator, Programmierer und den, der es werden will

`195 Seiten, CreateSpace 2013`

ISBN-13: 978-1489565990

Die Programmierung der eigene Webseite wird immer mehr zum Volkssport, und nicht wenige der Programmierer verdienen sich später ihr Brot oder zumindest ein Zubrot durch Programmieren der Webseiten anderer Leute. Leider kommt die Sicherheit der Webanwendung dabei häufig zu kurz, und auch in der Informatikerausbildung wird das Thema eher am Rande abgehandelt. Die Folge sind unnötige Schäden durch Hacker und Kriminelle.

Das Buch tritt an, vom der sorgfältigen Konfigurationsplanung des Server über die Auswahl geeigneter Programmierwerkzeuge, Verschlüsselungs- und Authentifizierungstechniken und Programmiermethoden bis hin zur Umgebung mit Firewall und Emailserver den Weg zum gesicherten Netzwerk aufzuzeigen. Alle Komponenten sind frei verfügbar, d.h. alles kann am eigenen Rechner ausführlich geübt und vertieft werden. Es eignet sich damit gleichermaßen für den Hobbyprogrammierer der eigenen Webseite, der sein Hobby zum Beruf ausbauen will, für den Studenten, der sich im Studium oder Selbststudium mit Serversicherheit beschäftigen will, bis hin zum Administrator kleiner (und mittlerer) Netzwerke, der Neues aufbaut oder vorhandenes einem Audit unterzieht.

Gilbert Brands

IT – Sicherheit 1.5

Internetprotokolle, Webprogrammierung,
Systemsicherheit

Wie funktionieren Internetprotokolle im Detail, welche Tricks können Angreifer
nutzen, um Informationen auszuspähen? Wie sind EMails, IP-Telefonie und Fun-
knetze organisiert, wie können Angreifer eindringen oder stören, wie kann man sich
schützen? Worauf ist bei der Webprogrammierung zu achten, um SQL-Injections,
Cross-Site-Scripting und andere Angriffe zu verhindern? Wie baut man ein ver-
schlüsseltes Netzwerk auf, was ist bei Zertifikaten zu beachten? Wie sind die Details
von SSL, SSH, PGP, VPN? Wie unterscheiden sich Public Key Infrastructure und
Kerberos? Das Buch gibt auf diese und weitere Fragen zu anderen Protokollen de-
taillierte Auskunft. Darüber hinaus werden Viren und Schadsoftware betrachtet
und Möglichkeiten der Absicherung angesprochen. Aber auch Geschäftsprozesse
wie Dokumentenverwaltung und anderes finden Berücksichtigung.

Das Buch wendet sich an Studenten Informatik und Wirtschaftsinformatik sowie
IT-Fachleute aus Unternehmen. Der Autor ist Hochschullehrer mit den Lehr- und
Forschungsgebieten softwaretechnische und mathematische IT-Sicherheit und
Mitglied   der   Arbeitsgruppe   IuK-Kriminalität   der   Polizeidirektion
Oldenburg/Hochschule Emden-Leer.

Ergänzend zu lesen: Verschlüsselung, Signaturen, Angriffsmethoden, ISBN
978-8448-0872-8. und Das C++ Kompendium, ISBN 978-3-642-04786-2.

- •Taschenbuch: 612 Seiten
- •Verlag: CreateSpace Independent Publishing Platform (29. November 2012)
- •Sprache: Deutsch
- •ISBN-10: 1481119273
- •ISBN-13: 978-1481119276
- •Link: http://www.amazon.de/dp/1481119273

(in German)

Pressemitteilung / Bibliotheksinformation

Buchneuerscheingung

Gilbert Brands

Verschlüsselung, Signaturen, Angriffsmethoden

Die Welt der elektronischen Sicherheit in Theorie und Praxis

BoD Norderstedt 2012, 596 Seiten, 45,80 €

ISBN 978-3-8448-0872-8

Das Buch beginnt mit der Untersuchung der Schnittstelle Mensch-Maschine. Wie sollten Kennworte unter verschiedenen Rahmenbedingungen gestaltet und verwaltet werden, warum ist beispielsweise eine vierstellige EC-PIN relativ sicher? Wie funktionieren biometrische Verfahren zur Personenidentifizierung, und wie sicher oder unsicher sind sie? Es geht dann über zu maschinengebundenen Verschlüsselungsverfahren und vergisst auch die für die Praxis wichtige Kodierungsfrage nicht. Über einfache Sicherungsverfahren und Wasserzeichen geht es zu symmetrischen Verschlüsselungsverfahren mit der Vorstellung der wichtigsten Algorithmen aus Netzwerk-, Festplatten- und Mobilfunkverschlüsselung, wobei ausführlich statistische und physikalische Angriffsverfahren vorgestellt werden. Mit der gleichen Sorgfalt werden die Hashalgorithmen der derzeitigen und der nächsten Generation und ihre vielfältige Verwendung vorgestellt, wobei auch hier Angriffsmöglichkeiten und ihre Ausnutzung nicht fehlen.

Für die asymmetrischen Verfahren wie RSA und Diffie-Hellman wird die Mathematik in einem eigenen Kapitel vorbereitet. Neben dem Standardeinsatz SSL oder PKI werden unterschiedliche Gruppensignaturen sowie auch die Möglichkeit der transparenten Durchführung demokratischer Wahlen über das Internet ausführlich vorgestellt. Die letzten beiden Kapitel widmen sich mit mathematischen Betrachtungen zu Primzahlen den noch offenen Fragen der asymmetrischen Algorithmen und mit der Untersuchung verschiedener Faktorisierungsalgorithmen der Sicherheitsfrage von RSA.

Das mathematische Niveau des Buches erfordert in den praxisorientierten Kapiteln kaum mehr als Schulniveau, gewinnt aber in den letzten Kapiteln einiges an Fahrt, wobei darauf Wert gelegt wird, dass der Leser den Anschluss nicht verliert. Dazu tragen auch die in jedem Kapitel reichlich vorhandenen Aufgaben bei, die den Leser meist auffordern, das Gelesene in eine Computeranwendung umzusetzen. Interesse an Programmierung ist daher auch gefragt.

Die Zielgruppen des Buches sind hauptsächlich Informatiker, Mathematiker und Elektrotechniker, und hier nicht nur Studenten und Hochschulen, sondern auch Praktiker im Beruf, die sich mit Sicherheitsfragen in Netzwerken oder der Entwicklung von Sicherheitsanwendungen auseinander setzen. Aber auch der einfach nur interessierte Leser dürfte auf seine Kosten kommen. Einen Eindruck über das Gesamtspektrum des Buches bietet der von den großen Online-Buchhändlern angebotene „Blick ins Buch".

http://www.amazon.de/Verschl%C3%BCsselung-Signaturen-Angriffsmethoden-elektronischen-Sicherheit/dp/3844808728/ref=sr_1_1?ie=UTF8&qid=1334637490&sr=8-1

Kontakt: Prof. Dr. Gilbert Brands, 26736 Krummhörn, email: gilbert@gilbertbrands.de

(in German)

Das C++ Kompendium

Taschenbuch: 950 Seiten

•**Verlag:** Springer; Auflage: 2. Aufl. 2010
(20. August 2010)

•**Sprache:** Deutsch

•**ISBN-10:** 3642047866

•**ISBN-13:** 978-3642047862

Das Lehrbuch vermittelt die zentralen Konzepte der Programmierung in C++ im Detail. Anhand komplexer Problemstellungen
wird gezeigt, wie korrekter und wiederverwendbarer Code entwick-
elt wird und wie sich mithilfe einer Programmiertechnik typische
Fehler vermeiden lassen. Leser werden anhand von Aufgaben schrit-
tweise an Problemstellungen herangeführt. Die mathematische und
algorithmische Herangehensweise macht das Buch auch zu einem
wertvollen Studienbegleiter für Veranstaltungen wie „Algorithmen
und Datenstrukturen" oder „numerische Mathematik".

Einführung in die Quanteninformatik

Taschenbuch: 384 Seiten

•Verlag: Springer; Auflage: 2011 (31. August 2011)

•Sprache: Deutsch

•ISBN-10: 3642206468

•ISBN-13: 978-3642206467

Ausgehend von der Theorie und den Protokollen der Quantenkryptografie werden in dem Band die Servicequalitäten vorgestellt, die angesichts der aktuellen technischen Möglichkeiten erreichbar sind. Unter Berücksichtigung wenig beachteter Gesichtspunkte der Kryptoanalyse diskutiert der Autor die erreichbare Sicherheit und untersucht die Möglichkeiten des Quantencomputing. Anhand praxisnaher Aufgaben können Leser ihr Wissen vertiefen und lernen, die Techniken kritisch zu bewerten. Mit Programmieranleitung für Simulationsversuche auf dem eigenen Rechner.